Victorian Authors and their Works

Victorian Authors and their Works

REVISION MOTIVATIONS AND MODES

Edited by
Judith Kennedy

OHIO
UNIVERSITY PRESS
ATHENS

Printed in the United States of America

95 94 93 92 91 5 4 3 2 1

All Ohio University Press books are printed on acid-free paper

Library of Congress Cataloging-in-Publication Data

Victorian authors and their works : revision motivations and modes / edited by Judith Kennedy.

p. cm.

Includes bibliographical references and index.

ISBN 0-8214-0976-X (alk. paper)

1. English literature—19th century—Criticism, Textual.

I. Kennedy, Judith, 1941-

PR468.T48V5 1991

820.9′008—dc20 91-324

CIP

Designed by Laury A. Egan

Contents

Preface

Judith Kennedy

The recent surge of interest in textual scholarship and its importance to modern literary criticism has resulted in a growing recognition among scholars that there are no "definitive" editions of works of literature; rather readers may select from various versions of a text, from a facsimile of the first or a subsequent publication of a work to any of several different modern "critical" editions of it. Besides resulting in a broader acknowledgment among scholars of ultimate textual indeterminacy, this new interest has also led to an increased awareness of the broad spectrum of influences or conditions, both personal and public, that may affect the creation and subsequent revisions of a text. The articles in this collection illustrate some of the forces (often totally unexpected, complex, or subtle) that came into play during the creation or revision of a selection of texts by Victorian authors. None of these articles attempts to present the complete process of revision that resulted in a particular text, because the total process, of course, is undiscoverable; instead each essay focuses upon one or a limited number of forces that influenced the motivations of an author and/or a mode of revision employed for a particular edition.

A BRIEF OVERVIEW OF THE STATE OF TEXTUAL CRITICISM AT THE PRESENT TIME

The most important modern theories and methodologies in the disciplines of bibliographical and textual studies were developed in the works of W. W. Greg, R. B. McKerrow, and Fredson Bowers, three of the best-known theorists and critical editors of the 1950s and 1960s, but today, many of the early rationales of establishing the history of texts and the editing of them have been modified, developed, or opposed by more recent critics of various orientations and emphases. Some of the critics who have brought fresh ideas to these disciplines include Peter Shillingsburg, Tom Davis, Mary Louise Pratt, Hans Walter Gabler, Philip Gaskell, Charlton Hinman, Morse Peckham, Peter Shaw, James Thorpe, Vinton Dearing, Don McKenzie, Steven Mailloux, Michael Warren, Steven Urkowitz, Donald Pizer, Hershel Parker, and Jerome McGann.

Notwithstanding the important reevaluations from these and other scholars who are developing the new textual criticism, most scholars in bibliography and textual studies recognize the more conservative G. Thomas Tanselle as one of the most knowledgeable and consistently logical experts in textual studies and are aware of the central role he has played in establishing some order in scholarly editing (especially through his work for the Modern Language Association of America Committee on Scholarly Editing and the Center for Editions of American Authors). Because of this recognition of Tanselle's work, his long-standing relationship with these important committees, and his influential role in the recent past as president of both the Bibliographical Society of America and the Guggenheim Foundation, today's critics generally consider and frequently must respond to his positions. On the other hand, Tanselle, who has developed many of the guidelines of scholarly editing and has made clear objections to some of the premises or methodologies of the new approaches, recognizes that the very innovation and controversy in the works of such critics as Jerome McGann, for instance, have stimulated interest in important, basic, but frequently ignored relationships, such as those between selecting a version of a text and the subsequent criticism of it.

Modern scholars of textual criticism are currently interested in many text-related issues, some of traditional and perennial concern, ranging from the central importance of selecting a copy text to deciding on the normalization or modernization of its language. Other significant issues include deciding on a rationale for editing a particular work and whether, how, or where to acknowledge editorial methodology in a new edition; presenting the publication history of the particular work being edited; providing information on the availability of its other versions; determining the extent of the accompanying apparatus (lists of variants, how hyphenation is handled, and other items of this nature); deciding on the kind and quantity of background information—historical, political, social, philosophical, or linguistic—i.e., data about a text's contextual situation that might be included with a new edition; establishing the relationship of a text to other texts of its kind; and exploring the intersubjectivity of a text and the responses of particular readers.

But perhaps a major interest of textual critics today and the one most relevant to the following articles involves developing a point of view toward a text as either a private or a public work. For instance, a basic decision an editor must make is whether to aim to represent the individual author's "final intent" or to incorporate the emendations of friends, editors, publishers, and others whose influence affected a written product. As editors and critics study the history of texts, they may gain insights into an author's internal or personal motivations or the influence of external or public forces (family, friends, editors, critics, and the broad book-purchasing audience) at a particular moment in the continually adjusting interplay of all such possible sources of revision. Thus the recent research and theories of the new textual criticism, besides dispelling the notion of a "definitive text," have created a widespread interest in the complex processes involved in literary creativity, from the earliest beginnings of a composition through its latest revised version. It is not surprising that the histories of the composition and revisions of particular texts have begun to interest a broader audience of composition theorists as well as literary scholars. Interest among composition scholars has been further stimulated because some critics, such as Hershel Parker, have raised issues concerning the creative impulse and how it may, however tentatively and speculatively, be observed or reflected in the composition and revision practices of particular authors. Textual scholarship, therefore, is also becoming a new source of information, theory, and ultimately, perhaps, experimentation in the teaching of the writing process to students of English.

ABOUT THIS COLLECTION

Because of the importance and originality of the scholarship in these articles, they will engage textual scholars and literary critics, particularly of the Victorian era. And composition specialists may also be interested in the discussions in these essays of the complexities of the writing experience and the many factors that affect it. The papers in this collection analyze the writing experiences of authors whose works span almost the entire nineteenth century. Almost all of our contributors have worked closely and extensively with manuscripts (which often included new or previously unpublished findings), and most have either written biographical studies on their subjects or edited recent editions of the works they discuss. While all of the articles are unencumbered by esoteric jargon, they demonstrate the broad variety of approaches taken by modern scholars in interpreting the composition and revision of texts. Some of the articles provide a more complete history of textual change and offer more specific examples of a thesis than other more generalizing or speculative selections that just begin to open issues, that offer theories that need to be further explored and discussed. The theses presented in these essays, whether heavily documented or highly speculative, provide some tentative breakthroughs in understanding individual writing processes and will stimulate further study of the issues they raise.

In "Inner and Outer Flame: Carlyle as Reviser," Fred Kaplan, Carlyle biographer and editor of the University of California Press edition of *The French Revolution,* sees the historian as basically a "non-reviser" in this work. As part of his argument, Kaplan offers the theory that Carlyle looked upon his writing as the embodiment of holy truth—and hated to change anything. He sees Carlyle's "revisions" rather as accretions. For example, Carlyle's awareness of new information did not usually result in revisions in subsequent editions of *The French Revolution*; Kaplan illustrates how Carlyle would leave erroneous information intact in a new edition, add the newly discovered contradictory facts to the text, and leave it for the reader to choose between them. Kaplan also offers speculations about the interplay between Carlyle's memory and creative abilities.

Susan Shatto's article, "The Textual Genesis of *Maud,*" discusses some broad characteristics of Tennyson's revisions of this work, which included eliminating elements that provided a fuller characterization of Maud as well as of other minor characters and plot developments in the love story. Furthermore, as Maud recedes in subsequent revisions, the character of the narrator is more fully developed. As Shatto interprets the poem, it evolves from a drama to a chamber drama of the narrator's own mind.

Carlyle's creation of *The French Revolution* and Tennyson's of *Maud* provide dramatic contrasts in the extent and differing processes of revision apparent in these particular works. Other authors develop very individualized systems or habits that affect their revision processes throughout a whole segment of their canon. For instance, in "Revision and the Pre-Raphaelite Text," Frederick Kirchhoff analyzes general patterns of revision in two major Pre-Raphaelite poets, Rossetti and Morris. Because both are acknowledged artists in the two modalities of poetry and painting, Kirchhoff studies how each of the poet-artist's working experience in one medium influenced the other. He also notes some vastly different overall dynamics at work in Rossetti and Morris in their approaches to both media.

Catherine Golden also explores an author-artist's revision practices in two modalities in "Retrieving Beatrix Potter's Revision Process." Golden studies the extent and variety of "retrieval practices" throughout Potter's storybook series. Potter used a rigorous strategy for textual and graphic revision "originally instilled by her Victorian publishers and increasingly by her own, often opposing, impulses." For instance, for her illustrations, Potter developed a "superimposition technique" similar to modern collage through which she could retain material reluctantly "cut" during revision. Also, Potter retrieved textual material deleted during revision and used it as a composing source for her new tales.

Not only do individual authors make decisions or intuitively follow patterns when they compose and revise literary works but many also take particular care to reorder their collected works in new editions. George Bornstein, for instance, in "'It is myself that I remake': W. B. Yeats's Revisions to His Early Canon," identifies an essential significance in the meaning of Yeats's recasting of large units in subsequent editions of his work. Bornstein offers a fascinating interpretation of Yeats's careful reordering of poems by citing an interplay between a particular ordering and Yeats's reconstruction of the image of the poet's persona that he wants the collection to reflect at a particular time. Bornstein believes that Yeats's construction of an edition reflects a process rather than a product: Yeats's continuous remaking of texts and thus of selves.

The above-mentioned essays concentrate upon the impetus of an individual author's personal motivations in affecting revisions. Critics who are currently advocating that literary works are not the products of isolated creative experiences but rather of the collaborative efforts of authors and those who react to a work and suggest revisions (relatives, friends, editors, critics, publishers, or audiences) will be particularly interested in other essays in this collection that focus upon this broader interplay in the process of revision. For instance, in "The Evolution of Henley's *In Hospital,*" Edward H. Cohen studies Henley's process of revising this poem over fifteen years. Cohen documents instances of Henley's reactions and resistance to the critical input of friends, editors, publishers and critics, such as Leslie Stephen, Robert Louis Stevenson, and John Blackwood. Some of their advice concerned broad stylistic elements of the poem, and these friends-editors-publishers-critics often encouraged Henley to become more closely aware of audience expectations and preferences at a particular time.

Other articles also deal with the effect, or at times, surprising lack of effect, other individuals had upon an author and a particular work. Although at one point in "Browning and How He Worked in Good Temper," Ashby Bland Crowder notes ironically Browning's attentive response to a particular critical reaction to his poem, the thrust of his essay is to demonstrate how Browning kept a generally composed mind, controlling his emotions during his revisions of "Pacchiarotto and How He Worked in Distemper" to attain his aesthetic and artistic goals. Crowder documents how the poet's successive revisions of this work went beyond the release of pent-up anger as Browning carefully worked to clarify ideas, elaborate the satire, add effective detail, eliminate deadwood, and improve metrics and sound effects in the poem.

Two other Victorian authors, Matthew Arnold and Thomas Hardy, responded in different ways to the expectations of prospective readers (both their popular audiences and critics) during the revision of their respective prose works. In "Approaching Truth 'on One Side after Another': Revision in the Religious Prose of Matthew Arnold," Suzanne O. Edwards illustrates how Arnold continued to defend or elaborate his views in both revisions and derivative articles that extend his arguments. Subsequent acts of prose composition entailed a "re-vision" of what he had written before, a reevaluation frequently prompted by critical reaction to his ideas or his presentations of them. Edwards interprets that Arnold's expansive sequences of essays reveal his responsiveness to his audience, especially his attempts to elaborate and extend arguments he had already presented but which his readers had somehow misunderstood, and she illustrates his practice of revising his previous compositions at virtually every opportunity.

In contrast, in "Hardy's Retroactive Self-Censorship: The Case of *The Well-Beloved*," Anne Pilgrim discusses very different dynamics of motivation and process in Hardy's reactions to his audience. Centrally, Hardy revised the original serial text of *The*

Well-Beloved when it appeared in book form in 1897 to remove elements that might give offense to the Victorian public on the eve of his return to poetry. Rather than clarification or elaboration of his original ideas or themes in this work, Hardy's complex motivations for revision involved the interplay of his financial concerns; his reactions to the furor surrounding the publication of *Jude the Obscure*; his desire to avoid false imputations of lack of originality because of the story's resemblance to *Jude* as well as to Richard Le Gallienne's 1896 novel, *The Quest of the Golden Girl*; and his intentions to conciliate both his wife and his public, who had been offended by the attacks on marriage and the sexual candor in *Jude*. Thus Pilgrim interprets Hardy's revisions as motivated by expediency and as part of his continual efforts at management of his career and reputation.

In another study of the serial-to-book development of a text, Linda K. Hughes studies Patmore's revisions from serial form to the last book edition of *Angel in the House* and discovers a pattern in the representation of woman in the evolution of this work. In "Entombing the Angel: Patmore's Revision of *Angel in the House*," Hughes notes significant relationships between the essential nature of revisions and important biographical developments in Patmore's life. The sense of women as living presences changes as they become "far more disembodied and reified, far more relegated to the status of symbols." Hughes clearly and extensively traces the process through which the female becomes "entombed, drained of life and vitality, and encased in form," and suggests that this phenomenon is related to the literal entombment of Patmore's first wife, Emily, after the first edition appeared. But Hughes proceeds to connect this mode of revision to larger issues involving publication format and the dynamics of revision itself. She sees Patmore returning to his poem as to an "artwork, an object which could be changed, modified, and manipulated to achieve greater refinement and beauty *as* an object." Similarly, the woman becomes emptied of vitality and presence and likewise acquires a status more closely identified with a beautiful object. In addition, Hughes offers the intriguing speculation of a relation between Patmore's increasing control of the text and increasing control over the female image.

In the next essay, David Leon Higdon documents the extensive revisions made by an editor (possibly Robert Garnett but more likely someone at Methuen) who effectively "restyled" *Under Western Eyes* in its transformation from serial to book form. In "Conrad, *Under Western Eyes,* and the Mysteries of Revision," Higdon clearly traces stages of authorial composition, revision, and editing that coexisted during the revision process and illustrates how the text became "contaminated" by its editors. Higdon's article focuses upon "how a uniform and consistent system of spelling, capitalization, and punctuation was imposed on Conrad's text," a system which is "preserved in the later English and American editions even though it bore no relationship to Conrad's lighter, looser, and generally satisfactory system."

The collection concludes with an article by John R. Reed, "Betrachtungen eines Uneditorialischen; or Editorial Thoughts of an Uneditorial Man," which begins by challenging readers to consider revision in the context of literary gestation itself. Reed questions the validity of any assumptions about the temporal linearity of a literary composition, including of course all its revisions, and reminds us that there is always an unrecorded "pre-text" not bound to a necessary temporal pattern. In addition, Reed opens the issue of problems posed by authors who write and then revise (and thereby perhaps permanently delete stages of revision) on computers, a situation scholars may need to consider when editing or criticizing modern works developed in this way.

It is hoped that the issues and theories in this collection will stimulate further interest and controversy in the study of texts. Whether or not one agrees with the various theses or methodologies offered in individual papers, the articles en masse begin to suggest the vast complexity of the revision process and the problems in accurately representing the composition and revision of a particular text; they indicate but a few of numerous interrelationships created by internal-personal and external-public influences upon authors and their works.

1

Inner and Outer Flame: Carlyle as Reviser

Fred Kaplan

My two favorite Victorian writers, Dickens and Carlyle, had different tendencies across their careers in regard to revising their manuscripts. The evidence from the extant manuscripts of Dickens's novels, of which there are many, reveals that he became more and more of a self-reviser beginning with *Dombey and Son*. The extant fragments of early novels show Dickens in the writing process as self-confidently nonreflective, certain that he had gotten it right the first time. But the manuscript of his last completed novel, *Our Mutual Friend*, is an interlinear arabesque of cryptic crossouts and alternate versions. Dickens gradually defined himself as an artist-craftsman for whom the process of writing was the experience of playing with language until the game was refined into artistic self-definition.

Carlyle began his writing career (and ended it) with the belief that his writing, like his speech, should be the visible embodiment of holy truth. For this reason, and for others, he hated to change a word. To the extent that the writing process was a process it was implosive, the deeper and deeper pursuit of truth, embodied in the narrative and in the gradual exploration of the self that the narrative contained. In general, throughout his writing career, he did not make substantial changes on his manuscripts or on his proofsheets. The changes tended to be of the accidental, nonsubstantive kind. Sometimes he made substantive crossouts and provided alternatives, but not frequently. This can be stated with some confidence, even though in Carlyle's case, a comparatively small amount of manuscript has survived. If only, like Dickens, he had made presents of whole manuscripts to friends, especially to John Forster, who would have taken as good care of Carlyle's manuscripts as he did of Dickens's. Neither Dickens nor Carlyle had much sense of his manuscripts having monetary value; for example, the frugal Jane Carlyle gave away the manuscript of *The French Revolution*, page by page as gifts to friends and acquaintances.

Unlike Dickens, Carlyle tended to embed into his completed text any substantial changes that he felt compelled to make—the revision process was the process of addition or accretion. He did not like to choose between alternatives. And if he made a factual error, which he sometimes admitted to have done, he was more likely to take the opportunity of a new edition to add corrective material, to supplement rather than to replace the existing text. The best example is his two accounts in *The French Revolution* of the sinking of the *Venguer.* In 1838 he became convinced, on the basis of evidence heretofore unknown to him, that his account in the first edition was inaccurate. He did not alter the original version but added a paragraph to the second British and American editions. This practice resulted partly from his conviction that the development of a narrative, of any writing, is a sacred process in which it is sacrilegious to tamper with the words—for the word is the spirit—and a true or sincere personal and/or public history is a record of the manifestations of the holy spirit which abides in the language of truth.

In Carlyle's case, as for most of us, reasons of principle that can be abstracted into philosophy had their deep roots in personality. He was an impatient man, who always liked to look backward but never liked to go backward; he never liked to go over the same ground twice. He had to do so, sometimes; he recognized that. Intellectually, his range was sufficiently limited so that he had little choice but to repeat his message. But by temperament he was not made for the long haul or the word-by-word, time-consuming refinement of one stage of writing into another. He felt most comfortable with writing at white-hot intensity and rapidly—that was the stage of drama and excitement and fulfillment. After that stage, he lost emotional interest. The pleasure decreased considerably. And, despite his occasional claim to the contrary, he himself did not like doing painful things, or, to put it another way, one of the painful things he did not like doing was rewriting or revising. He liked to get a book over with as rapidly as possible, and once the first draft was done, he preferred, he was almost compelled, to insist and to find reasons to justify his insistence that the book was done and not to be tampered with, except to be added to, if necessary.

How especially painful to him, then, was the destruction in March 1835 of the manuscript of the first volume of *The French Revolution.* An abbreviated, somewhat dramatic account of that notorious episode would relate: the lending of the manuscript to John Stuart Mill; the conflicting accounts of where the manuscript was destroyed; the charged atmosphere of pain and despair on that Friday night on which Mill, "pale and distraught," told the Carlyles about its destruction, while his "Platonic Innamorata" waited outside in the carriage; and then Carlyle's own tortured account of his initial despair, which led to his claim the next morning that "I was as a little schoolboy who had laboriously written his *Copy* as he could, and was shewing it not without satisfaction to the Master: but . . . the master had suddenly torn it, saying: 'No, boy, thou must go and write it better.'"[1] My concern here, however, is not with the narrative as a whole but with one fascinating aspect of the episode that throws interesting, curious, even perplexing light on Carlyle as a reviser.

The challenge Carlyle faced was an immense one, particularly given how intensely he disliked revision and/or going back over the same ground; the "Master," like a monitor of artistic conscience, had told him, so he imagined, that he must do it better. As an artist—as a writer—Carlyle could, when forced to, as he now was, admit that it could be done better. But as the full personality, which contained so much more than his recognition of this, came to bear on the situation and he began to rewrite, he had the constant sense that what he was creating now was noticeably inferior to what had been destroyed. Of course, he was not revising. There was no extant manuscript to revise. Was he rewriting? Only, he claimed, in the sense that he was doing the same task over again, using the same materials to produce a replacement for what had been destroyed. For, he claimed, there was no extant version of what that manuscript had contained: there was no earlier draft, there were no pre-manuscript fragments or notes. There were his books; they had underlinings and probably, though this isn't certain, some marginal comments. But the only hard copy, so to speak, had been destroyed, and the soft copy consisted of electronic pulses of mind and memory, patterns in his mind.

But this is not entirely accurate, though accurate enough both in its emotional and practical resonances. Years after the event Carlyle remarked "that my poor manuscript, all except some four tattered leaves," had been "annihilated." Apparently four brief fragments of the original manuscript, that is manuscript one, of *The French Revolution,* did survive. Only one of those "four tattered leaves" is known to exist now, and it consists of two eight-line fragments, occupying two sides of a single, singed, torn portion of a page. It is a perplexing, fascinating document. For the fragment contains material and phrasing perplexingly similar to but also interestingly different from corresponding passages in Volume I, Book VII, Chapter iv, "The Menads," and Volume I, Book VII, Chapter v, "Usher Maillard," in the first edition, which is, we presume, based on the new manuscript.[2] In fact, the narrative sequences and some of the phrasing in the charred fragments from the destroyed original manuscript and in the first edition are identical. This first edition was printed from a new manuscript, of course, written, Carlyle claimed, without benefit of any portion of the first manuscript in front of him. His claim implies that not even the "four tattered leaves" were used, though even if he had had them on his desk, the practical exigencies of composition would have made it difficult for him suddenly to insert them at some appropriate point. For he would have had to write backward from the tattered leaves to create chapters into which they would fit, and that was not how Carlyle worked, and his own account of the creation of a new manuscript of Volume I shows that he created the new manuscript as if he always had a blank page in front of him. The passages in the first edition that correspond to the surviving fragment from the original manuscript are considerably expanded and altered. But the narrative sequence and the phrasing are sufficiently similar (sometimes indeed identical) to raise numbers of interesting questions about Carlyle as a writer and as a reviser and even some broader questions about the accepted account of the creation of the new manuscript of the first volume.

These questions are best raised with both sides of the tattered leaf and the corresponding passages in the first edition clearly in view.

1. Side A of the leaf (Figure 1.1)
2. Side B of the leaf (Figure 1.2)
3. *The French Revolution* (1837), Volume I, Book VII, Chapter iv, p. 353 (Figure 1.3)
4. *The French Revolution* (1837), Volume I, Book VII, Chapter v, pp. 356–7 (Figure 1.4)

The similarities are striking, but the differences are also noticeable. The obvious questions are:

1. Is this leaf, which scholars have claimed is from the burnt manuscript and which is so labeled at the Carlyle House in Chelsea, really from the original manuscript or is it a fragment from the new manuscript? If so, then the revisions on manuscript and the changes from the manuscript to the first edition are interesting, atypical, and unusual examples of Carlyle at work revising himself. There is, though, some strong though not conclusive physical evidence that the leaf comes from the original. For example, there are burn or char marks on it.

2. If it is from the original manuscript, did Carlyle have it in front of him when creating the new manuscript and incorporate phrases from it into the new manuscript?

3. And, following this line of thought, is it possible that Carlyle had even more—much more—of the original manu-

script in front of him when writing the new manuscript? There is evidence to conclude that he did not, including his own claims. But it is not conclusive evidence.

4. If this leaf is from the original, as I believe it is, then it is possible that Carlyle had in his memory what would be to us a prodigious amount of the destroyed original manuscript, so much of it that he was able to create a new manuscript strikingly close to the original not only in structure and in narrative development but even in regard to the materials that appeared in paragraphs and in the phrasing and diction within paragraphs.

Of course, the Victorians placed much more emphasis than we do on the training of the memory from early childhood education onward. No doubt Carlyle had a trained memory. But if my speculation here is correct, he would have had also what we these days call a photographic memory, though what that is precisely I am not certain. If that means that one recalls exactly what one has previously read, then indeed that is not what Carlyle had or at least did in this case. But undoubtedly he had a powerful memory, and it is not beyond reasonable possibility that he wrote the new manuscript partly as the re-creation of recall and partly as new creation, what we might think of as a powerful interaction between memory and desire.

NOTES

1. A fuller, more detailed and documented account of these events appears in Fred Kaplan, *Thomas Carlyle, Biography* (Ithaca, N.Y.: Cornell University Press, 1983), pp. 217–22.

2. Thomas Carlyle, *The French Revolution: A History,* 3 vols. (London: James Fraser, 1837) 1:353, 356–57.

Figure 1.1: Scrap of the burnt manuscript of *The French Revolution* (the only piece known to be in existence)

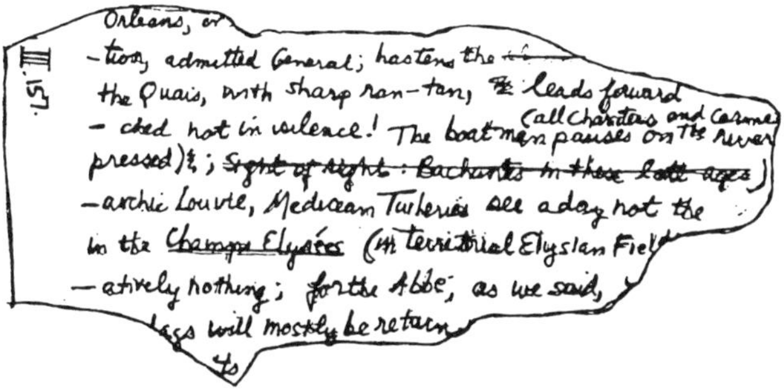

*Photograph of "The Charred Scrap" of *The French Revolution* reproduced with permission from Carlyle's House, The National Trust

Figure 1.2: Scrap of the burnt manuscript of *The French Revolution*

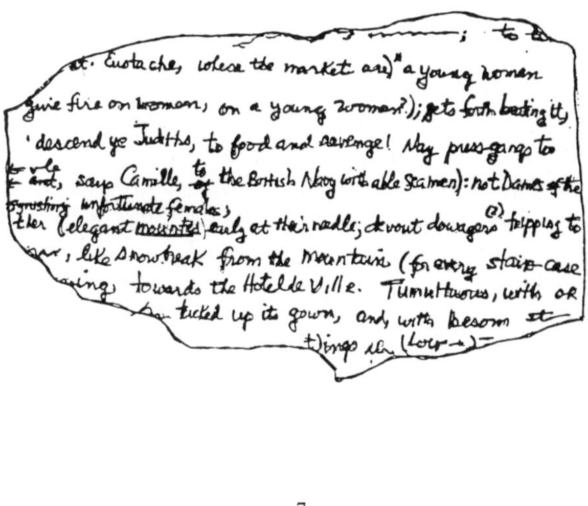

Figure 1.3: From a first edition copy of Thomas Carlyle's *The French Revolution* (1837), Volume I, Book VII, Chapter iv, p. 353

THE MENADS. 353

A thought, or dim raw-material of a thought, was fermenting all night, universally in the female head, and might explode. In squalid garret, on Monday morning, Maternity awakes, to hear children weeping for bread. Maternity must forth to the streets, to the herb-markets and Bakers'-queues; meets there with hunger-stricken Maternity, sympathetic, exasperative. O we unhappy women! But, instead of Bakers'-queues, why not to Aristocrats' palaces, the root of the matter? *Allons*! Let us assemble. To the Hôtel-de-Ville; to Versailles; to the Lanterne!

In one of the Guardhouses of the Quartier Saint-Eustache, 'a young woman' seizes a drum,—for how shall National Guards give fire on women, on a young woman? The young woman seizes the drum; sets forth, beating it, 'uttering cries relative to the dearth of 'grains.' Descend, O mothers; descend, ye Judiths, to food and revenge!—All women gather and go; crowds storm all stairs, force out all women: the female Insurrectionary Force, according to Camille, resembles the English Naval one; there is a universal 'Press of women.' Robust Dames of the Halle, slim Mantua-makers, assiduous, risen with the dawn; ancient Virginity tripping to matins; the Housemaid, with early broom; all must go. Rouse ye, O women; the laggard men will not act; they say, we ourselves may act!

And so, like snowbreak from the mountains, for every staircase is a melted brook, it storms; tumultuous, wild-shrilling, towards the Hôtel-de-Ville. Tumultuous; with or without drum-music: for the Faubourg Saint-Antoine also has tucked up its gown; and, with besom-staves, fire-irons, and even rusty pistols

Figure 1.4: From a first edition copy of Thomas Carlyle's *The French Revolution* (1837), Volume I, Book VII, Chapter v, pp. 356–7.

356

CHAPTER V.

USHER MAILLARD.

In flames, truly,—were it not that Usher Maillard, swift of foot, shifty of head, has returned!

Maillard, of his own motion, for Gouvion or the rest would not even sanction him,—snatches a drum; descends the Porch-stairs, ran-tan, beating sharp, with loud rolls, his Rogues'-march: To Versailles! *Allons; à Versailles!* As men beat on kettle or warmingpan, when angry she-bees, or say, flying desperate wasps, are to be hived; and the desperate insects hear it, and cluster round it,—simply as round *a* guidance, where there was none: so now these Menads round shifty Maillard, Riding-Usher of the Châtelet. The axe pauses uplifted; Abbé Lefevre is left half-hanged; from the belfry downwards all vomits itself. What rub-a-dub is that? Stanislas Maillard, Bastille-hero, will lead us to Versailles? Joy to thee, Maillard; blessed art thou above Riding-Ushers! Away then, away!

The seized cannon are yoked with seized cart-horses: brownlocked Démoiselle Théroigne, with pike and helmet, sits there as gunneress, 'with haughty eye 'and serene fair countenance;' comparable, some think, to the *Maid* of Orleans, or even recalling 'the idea of

'Pallas Athene.'* Maillard (for his drum still rolls) is, by heaven-rending acclamation, admitted General. Maillard hastens the languid march. Maillard, beating rhythmic, with sharp ran-tan, all along the Quais, leads forward, with difficulty, his Menadic host. Such a host—marched not in silence! The bargeman pauses on the River; all wagoners and coach-drivers fly; men peer from windows,—not women, lest they be pressed. Sight of sights: Bacchantes, in these ultimate Formalised Ages! Bronze Henri looks on, from his Pont-Neuf; the Monarchic Louvre, Medicean Tuileries see a day not theretofore seen.

And now Maillard has his Menads in the *Champs Elysées* (Fields *Tartarean* rather); and the Hôtel-de-Ville has suffered comparatively nothing. Broken doors; an Abbé Lefevre, who shall never more distribute powder; three sacks of money, most part of which (for Sansculottism, though famishing, is not without honour) shall be returned:† this is all the damage. Great Maillard! A small nucleus of Order is round his drum; but his outskirts fluctuate like the mad Ocean: for Rascality male and female is flowing in on him, from the four winds; guidance there is none but in his single head and two drumsticks.

O Maillard, when, since War first was, had General of Force such a task before him, as thou this day? Walter the Penniless still touches the feeling heart: but then Walter had sanction; had space to turn in; and also his Crusaders were of the male sex. Thou, this

* Deux Amis, iii. 157.

† Histoire Parlementaire, iii. 310.

2

The Textual Genesis of *Maud**

Susan Shatto

The textual history of *Maud*, compared to that of *In Memoriam*, is relatively uncomplicated to reconstruct: *Maud* is only a third as long as *In Memoriam;* it was composed in only eighteen months (with the exception of three poems composed in the 1830s); and a higher proportion survives of the original number of manuscripts.[1] The particular problem of reconstruction which *Maud* seems at first to pose is quickly resolved: this is the problem of attempting to reconcile the mass of conflicting secondary material—the testimony of Tennyson's friends and of Tennyson himself—which, until all the manuscripts became available for examination and publication in 1969, provided the only information about the genesis of the poem and its history of composition. Aside from the fact that some of the witnesses were either notoriously unreliable, or relied on their reminiscences, or were influenced by the testimony of other witnesses, or (in the case of Tennyson himself) were secretive, evasive, and forgetful (consciously or otherwise), none of the secondary material has the

*This essay is a synopsis of the introduction to *Tennyson's "Maud": A Definitive Edition*, edited with introduction and commentary by Susan Shatto (London: Athlone Press, 1986), pp. 1–38.

authority of the manuscripts. Now that the textual evidence is available, attempting to reconcile the discrepancies in the secondary material is not only a thankless task but also a side issue of scholarship which has little bearing on the process of reconstruction.

This is not to say that the testimony of Tennyson himself should be dismissed, merely considered cautiously and occasionally ignored. The reasons why are obvious, and they have to do both with the nature of the poem—*Maud* is more entirely and more intimately autobiographical than *In Memoriam*—and with the nature of the poet—a shy, arrogant man who often invited criticism but only accepted praise. He resented and rebuffed inquiries about his poetry—considering them hostile or stupid, or both—and covered his tracks with red herrings. Some of his statements about *Maud* not only conflict within themselves and among themselves but also with the evidence of the manuscripts. When confronted by such contradictions, the textual scholar ought to trust the tale more than the teller.

Fortunately, the statements of Tennyson and his friends agree with the evidence of the manuscripts in one respect: the germ of *Maud* was "Oh! that 'twere possible," the lyric which Tennyson published, with characteristic reluctance, in 1837. What made him turn his thoughts, in October 1853, to a poem essentially twenty years old no one knows for certain. Perhaps it had never been out of his thoughts, inspired as it was by the death of Arthur Hallam, echoed as it was in *In Memoriam*. What is certain is that by the spring of 1854, "Oh! that 'twere possible" had occasioned a small group of poems (or sections) which Tennyson was transcribing into two notebooks, one of which shows the sections arranged in a sequence of fair copies.

Like the trio of ship lyrics which became the first written sections of *In Memoriam*, this sequence constitutes the first written sections of *Maud*. All but one of the six sections are lyrics, but they are given a dramatic structure, beginning with the narrator meeting Maud in the woods and her acceptance of him. The penultimate section comprises the interpolated "Oh! that 'twere possible," and the final section comprises the present final part of the poem, Part III, showing the narrator recovered from his madness and inspired by the vision of Maud in a dream to go to war, his love for her becoming subsumed in the higher aim of love for his country.

This early sequence of sections constitutes a *Maud* in miniature: already the narrative line is established, including the climax and resolution, and the main figures are sketched, along with clues to the direction of the development of their characterizations and their relationships. Into this sequence Tennyson inserted three further sections the details of which are less important to relate than what the sections represent: they typify the nature of the additions he would make to the sequence as it developed further. Having established the framework of the story line and sketched the characters who would carry it out, his concerns henceforward would be to elaborate the plot, integrating and intertwining its elements; enrich the characterization; intensify the atmosphere; and increase the dramatic tension.

Various kinds of textual evidence suggest that Tennyson composed these sections between January and March 1854 and that by the late spring he had composed several more. It is at this point that we encounter some of the pieces of secondary material referred to earlier: Tennyson's well-known statements about the influence of Sir John Simeon on the genesis and composition of the poem. It is not necessary to rehearse this familiar story, merely to remind the reader that Tennyson's statements have always been understood to mean that Simeon instigated the composition of *Maud*—that Simeon was, to use the charming image of Ralph Rader, the "onlie begetter" of *Maud*,[2] and that none of the poem, or only Part III, had been composed by June 1854.

In fact, of course, the evidence of the manuscripts shows that Tennyson had composed and arranged a substantial number of sections long before he met Simeon. Why should he say, then, that it was Simeon who begged him to "weave story round this poem, and so *Maud* came into being"? Simply because before he met Simeon Tennyson very likely had no definite plan to publish the evolving sequence. The history of all his major volumes of poetry is the history of his reluctance to publish them. He had felt this way about *In Memoriam,* for example, when that sequence was substantially completed, and it was only the intervention of his publisher (and the offer of a large cheque) that determined him to complete the poem and publish it. To his publisher's inquiry if he had been writing anything of late with a view to publication, Tennyson emphatically replied, "No." When Moxon pressed him ("surely you have not been idle?"), Tennyson, with characteristic churlishness, said that "he had been writing for his own relief & private satisfaction some things that the public would have no interest in, and would not care to see." When Moxon asked to look at the manuscript, Tennyson gave him *In Memoriam.*[3]

Just as Tennyson needed his friends to suggest the subjects for him to write about, he needed his friends to urge him to publish. In the past, Arthur Hallam and James Spedding had been the chief providers of the necessary encouragement. Now, with *Maud*, it was the turn of John Simeon. Simeon's relationship to *Maud* was not that of "onlie begetter" but of midwife: he facilitated the emergence of the poem by prompting Tennyson to carry on developing the sequence started six months before and to publish it. Such a reconstruction of the events is supported by some details in the account of Simeon's daughter, who said that Tennyson told Simeon that "Oh! that 'twere possible" was "really intended to belong to a dramatic poem which he had never been able to carry out."[4] Tennyson was able to tell Simeon about the "dramatic poem" because months before they met he had already composed its framework, including numerous dramatic scenes. If Tennyson actually did also say that "he had never been able to carry out" the poem, this could not mean that he had lost the inspiration to compose further sections. The lyric sequence was a form so suited to his imagination that he could generate new lyrics, elaborating, developing, and prefacing what had gone before, as profusely as a reef of coral generates new branches. What he surely meant was that he had not felt compelled to complete the sequence, that he was content to allow it to develop at the pace of his own inclinations. The lack of confidence evident in the expression attributed to him recalls his self-deprecatory rejoinder to Moxon's inquiry about *In Me-*

moriam. Indeed, it is easy to imagine him replying to Simeon's inquiry with the same admission: "he had been writing for his own relief & private satisfaction some things that the public would have no interest in, and would not care to see." But the depth of his feelings for Simeon obviously strengthened Simeon's persuasiveness. Henceforward, Tennyson would devote himself to rounding out the established framework of the sequence and to integrating its parts. Hardly more than a year after their reacquaintance, he would be able to put the published poem into Simeon's hands.

The most interesting aspects of this final stage in the composition of the poem involve the direction of the poem's development, the nature of Tennyson's revisions, and the effect of these revisions on the characterization of Maud and the narrator. The early lyric sequence told a love story in which Maud and the narrator shared the foreground. Augmented by lyric prefaces and set pieces and by narrative links, the love story itself became the emotional germ of a poetic drama. The hitherto shadowy figures of the brother and rival lover were developed, and new minor characters were introduced. Subsidiary themes of a social nature were introduced to serve as a foil for the emotions generated in the narrator by his love for Maud. These themes also became the focus for the same kind of cynical, suspicious, and angry feelings which the narrator had expressed for Maud in some early drafts but which were toned down or revised out as the sequence developed. Other violent feelings were revised out but only in the later stages of composition.

As I have already indicated, Tennyson's concern in expanding the sequence was to complicate the plot and tighten the structure, increase dramatic tension, deepen character interest, and intensify atmosphere. The development of these elements combined to overshadow the character of Maud. A figure of stature in the early lyric sequence, she is gradually shouldered out of the foreground by the more individualized and active minor characters and, indeed, by the narrator himself. While the characterization of Maud recedes as the sequence develops, that of the narrator increases. The subsidiary themes and incidents which are introduced all provide a field for the narrator to display and play out his own character. A scene of great dramatic potential for example, the duel with the brother and his death, is displaced from the action so as not to distract from the real drama of the poem, the chamber drama of the narrator's own interiority.

What makes the minor characters of the brother, the rival lover, and the Peace orator more individualized than Maud is the fact that they are all invigorated by real-life originals: the brother by Tennyson's detested uncle, Charles Tennyson d'Eyncourt; the lover by d'Eyncourt's friend and Tennyson's enemy, Bulwer-Lytton; and the Peace orator by John Bright.

But what of Maud herself?—originally in the limelight but ultimately, comparatively, in the wings. Can she be identified with a particular individual? Tennyson's youthful relationships with Emily Sellwood, Sophy Rawnsley and Rosa Baring were first revealed by Sir Charles Tennyson's biography,[5] in his discussion of what he quaintly termed "Alfred's early love experiences." The influence these experiences may have had on the composition of *Maud* was ingeniously explored by Ralph Rader in *Tennyson's "Maud": The Biographical Genesis,* a landmark in Tennyson scholarship. In particular, Rader proposed Rosa Baring as the foremost model for Maud. To a lesser extent, he suggested, Sophy Rawnsley and Emily Sellwood also served as models.

In many respects, the case Rader puts is convincing. The autobiographical genesis of the poem is undeniable. *Maud* was to Tennyson what *David Copperfield* was to Dickens, his "favourite child," and for the same reason. What could be argued is that an insistence on specificity of identification not only narrows and flattens the character called Maud but also falsifies the essence of the poem.

From the earliest stages of composition onward, Maud is as idealized a figure as the subjects of "Claribel," "Lillian," "Isabel," "Margaret," "Madeline," and "Adeline"—Tennyson's early-girlie poems of the 1830s. The Dark Lady of the *Sonnets* and the Arthur of *In Memoriam* are more individualized as characters than the character of Maud. The indistinctness of her characterization suggests that her function in the poem is not as a character at all but as the obscure object of the narrator's desire. The intentional obscurity in the depiction of Maud is analogous to the ambiguous source of emotion in "Tears, idle tears, I know not what they mean." Considering the impregnable degree of Tennyson's self-absorption, it is difficult to believe that any woman, or synthesis of women, or indeed, anything external to Tennyson himself could have occasioned the composition of his "favourite child." The combined impact on *Maud* of his wide reading, his social and political passions, and even his feelings for those he had loved and lost was as nothing compared to the chief source of the poem and its primary influence: the depths and unreconciled complexities of his own self. Simply, he looked in his heart and wrote.

NOTES

1. A detailed account of the textual history of *Maud* appears in the introduction to *Tennyson's "Maud": A Definitive Edition*, ed. Susan Shatto (London: Athlone Press, 1986), pp. 1–38.

2. Ralph W. Rader, *Tennyson's "Maud": The Biographical Genesis* (Berkeley and Los Angeles: University of California Press, 1963), p. 10.

3. From an account by Charles Tennyson Turner, as reported by A. J. Symington, in a letter to Hallam Tennyson, 11 January 1894, in the Tennyson Research Center, Lincoln, England.

4. Louisa E. Ward, "Tennyson and Sir John Simeon, and Tennyson's Last Years," in *Tennyson and His Friends*, ed. Hallam Tennyson (London: Macmillan, 1911), pp. 308–9.

5. Charles Tennyson, *Alfred Tennyson* (New York: Macmillan, 1949).

3

Revision and the Pre-Raphaelite Text

Frederick Kirchhoff

Our fantasy of the magisterial writer may encourage us to imagine revision as an exercise in detachment, in which the writer who composed his first draft in the heat of inspiration returns to it with the objectivity and sure purpose of a copy editor. But in most cases revision is inseparable from the subjective experience of writing—inseparable from the poet's nagging sense of a certain fuzziness in a line of verse that cannot quite be brought into focus, from the novelist's triumphant perception of the autonomy of his characters, from the essayist's frustrated search for the exact words necessary to flesh out a skeletal conception. Whatever their other determinants—and there are many—these experiences are inevitably shaped by the writer's conception of his own activity—by his notion of what, practically speaking, one does when one sets about "creating literature" and his notion of the kind of work that validates one's right to be called a "poet" or "author."

If, for example, a poet believes that a poem should be a spontaneous record of visionary experience, then any alterations of a first draft would seem inappropriate—at best, a necessary evil, at worst, a deceit. If, on the other hand, a poet conceptualizes his work as a carefully wrought artifact, then the process of laboring to bring the text into completion is essential to his self-image. For such a writer, composing a first draft, however excellent, would have the feel of an unfinished activity, which only the act of revision, however trivial its effects, would close.

Within the extremes defined by these two naive positions one might locate a scattering of more sophisticated notions of literary revision. The Shelleyan model of composition, in which writing is conceived as a belated effort to memorialize inspiration, sees revision as an attempt to bring the text into closer conformity with its originating impulse. Although the process of revision may be infinite, it occurs in finite space, since the writer does not imagine himself altering or supplementing what he believes to be the meaning of the text. In contrast, the notion that the writer's conception of his work evolves through the act of writing, imagines revision as an act of artistic growth or discovery. By implication, only the (real or metaphoric) death of the writer would produce an unambiguously "final" version, for, in time, all apparently final versions turn out to have been provisional. (Wordsworth's *Prelude* presents an obvious example of this concept of revision, as do the collected poems of Yeats.)

I raise these issues as background to a question about the relationship between the process of writing and the process of graphic composition: To what extent might the artist-writer's working experience in one medium influence his notion of creative activity and therefore of revision in the other? My concern is not the historical problem of the influence of art on literature or of literature on art. I have no intention of entering the debate on whether Rossetti synthesized the sister arts or, as David Riede argues, promoted their independence.[1] Rather, I am concerned with the manner in which the experience of bringing a work of graphic art to completion might affect the artist-writer's practice of literary revison.

Let me suggest some possibilities. For the graphic artist, framing the space of composition is an initial decision that dictates features of the work that follows. Granted there may be preliminary sketching to solve problems of form and relationship, yet there is a significant gap between these initiatory activities and the practical commencement of, let us say, an oil painting. The size of the canvas chosen determines the size of the images that will be painted on it. Moreover, it defines a space that must be filled. The unfilled canvas is, literally, a sign that the work is incomplete—a sign particularly meaningful for the Pre-Raphaelite artist, with his dedication to accuracy in minute detail. (Ruskin confirms this view in his architectural watercolors, which use unfilled space to make the point that they are to be viewed as historical records, not as art.) Of course, working within a framed space not only determines what an artist *must* do; it also marks off areas he need not consider. The question of whether to extend the painting with a five-inch pennisula three inches below the upper righthand corner simply does not arise. Or, if it does, then it becomes a question of whether to start over from scratch.

One might expect an artist-writer, used to working within a rigorously predetermined space, to be comfortable with similarly enclosed literary forms. That Rossetti seems to have liked writing sonnets and narrative poems with strict stanzaic patterns is thus in keeping with his experience as a painter. Even his title *The House of Life* reflects this sense of literary form as an enclosed space.

Conversely, one might expect the artist-writer to resist literary revisions that violate the spatial outlines of his work. Rossetti was capable of making such revisions, but his 1879 letter to Hall Caine explaining the addition of new material to his poem "Sister Helen" suggests that he regarded this addition as a remarkable event. Oddly, he asserts that the text has been "much revised in detail" but not "in the main." Yet his own language contradicts this statement when he goes on to explain that "the first main addition to this poem was made by me only a few days ago:—eight stanzas, (six together and two scattered ones) involving a new incident!! Your hair is on end, I know, but if you heard the stanzas, they would smooth if not curl it. The gain is immense."[2] Elsewhere Rossetti is not adverse to adding lines or stanzas to poems, but these additions usually clarify or emphasize material already present in the text. What is notable in this instance is the addition of an entirely new episode.

The gain is, indeed, "immense." The new stanzas focus Helen's indeterminate revenge by locating it on the wedding day of the lover who has betrayed her, and the addition of his newlywed bride as a final suppliant, as Rossetti recognized, lifts "the tragedy to a yet sterner height." Yet he still feels the need to justify the addition and attributes to Caine his own surprise at having accomplished it.

The eight new stanzas were not Rossetti's only revisions of "Sister Helen." Janet Camp Troxell has traced the history of the text in detail from its 1854 appearance in the *Dusseldorf Artists' Album* to the 1881 collected edition of Rossetti's *Poems*.[3] His minute revisions illustrate Rossetti's characteristic, perhaps obsessive, habit of fussing over details. It is a habit particularly appropriate to a painter working in oils, who must allow his painted surface to dry before superimposing details and who therefore returns periodically to continue work on a given canvas. A writer used to this kind of "work" in painting is likely to take it for granted that a similar kind of "work" is appropriate to literary creation. Thus what may appear obsessive rewriting to us may to Rossetti have seemed standard practice.

The artistic value of this practice remains, however, in question. The first line in the second stanza of "Sister Helen," originally "And if ye have melted your wax aright," is altered in 1869 to "And if you have seethed your wax aright," and then, later the same year, to "But if you have done your work aright." One could argue that each of these changes is an improvement, but one could also construct an argument vindicating a different sequence of alterations. In fact, the ongoing act of revision constitutes a kind of play with the text—a trying out of expressions in search of the one that feels right. Another example from "Sister Helen" is Rossetti's experiment with successive proper names—Keith of Ewan, Keith of Ewerm, Holm of Ewern, Holme of Ewern, Weir of Ewern, Keith of Ewerm—in which the process of reaching an ultimate choice is a matter of trial and error rather than incremental improvement.

The difficulty in evaluating the trial-and-error method of revision is illustrated by Paull Franklin Baum's commentary on the changes Rossetti made between the 1847 and 1850 versions of "The Blessed Damozel."

> The choice of *damozel* for *damsel* was a happy inspiration; and the concomitant changes of "leaned out" for "against" and "gold" for "silver" were equally happy. The third and fourth lines were certainly not improved in 1850. Though the repetition of "robe" in line 9 from line 7 looks like a careless error, the "rose" worn on the neck (1850) is not altogether pleasing; and the first reading makes better sense and better grammar. "Terrace" for "rampart" is a good illustration of the infelicitous alterations of 1850; but on the other hand the new stanza vi, with its vivid images, is proof that Rossetti could perfectly well recover the feeling of the first draft.[4]

Whether one agrees with Baum on individual points, his equivocal judgment of Rossetti's revisions suggests the arbitrary nature of the poet's technique.

With hindsight, of course, one can usually invent an argument that explains why the final version of an extensively revised text is the best version. But the relationship between Rossetti's tinkering and his stature as a poet remains undecided. Recently, Robert Keane's claim that Rossetti's meticulous revisions of his poetry demonstrate the poet a "thorough craftsman"[5] has been challenged by David Sonstroem's reminder that "all care is not craftsmanship." But Sonstroem's view that "details of wording . . . are quite removed from Rossetti's central aesthetic strength"[6] has, in turn, been challenged by Joseph Gardner, who argues that Rossetti's revisions of the "Newborn Death" sonnets in *The House of Life* offer "unequivocal" evidence of the poet's "genuine craftsmanship."[7]

Overall, this fussing resulted in a greater density or richness of language and imagery, and in this respect Rossetti was following Keats's advice to "load every rift . . . with ore."[8] Because Rossetti shares this habit of revision with poets—like Keats—who are not also artists, there is no reason to attribute this aspect of Rossetti's revision process solely to his experience as a painter. Moreover, Rossetti's fussiness toward both his art and his poetry, like his reluctance to exhibit his paintings in public and his terror of negative criticism, can be explained as symptoms of a threatened, insecure image of the self. (Even his predilection for enclosed literary forms may be traced to his need for security.)

However, if an obsession with minute revisions does not in itself link his practice as a writer with his practice as an artist, the pattern of his revisions does suggest a link. The artist, who begins his work by laying out broad surfaces of color and then gradually overlays them with more and more precise details—which may themselves be covered over or reshaped—may encourage the poet to feel that a first draft defines the large units of form within which he will perform at intervals the task of revision. Revision, in other words, is conceived as superimposition rather than alteration or linear supplement.

As a process of literary revision, this habit is not merely a matter of modifying visual or auditory details. The most interesting aspect of Rossetti's 1879 additions to "Sister Helen" is the introduction of an element of plot necessary if we are to make narrative sense of the poem. In its earlier versions, the poem is like many of Rossetti's paintings, in which figures appear in circumstances that remain shadowy or uncertain—or in which, to put it another way, affective states are presented without a narrative context. In a few instances, such as his sequence of Proserpine representations, later versions of a painting attempt to clarify this narrative significance by adding written language to the painting. In "Sister Helen" this addition takes the form of a movement from vague situation to a clearly defined narrative sequence of events. In "The Blessed Damozel," another extensively revised poem, Rossetti's modifications not only emphasize "the apparently unbridgeable gulf that separates the heavenly maiden and the earthly lover"[9]; they also underline the narrative immediacy of the poem by redirecting our attention to the consciousness of the earthly lover. In its original form, the text encourages us to read it as a situation; in its final version, it presents itself clearly as an event. Similarly, in bringing together the sonnets he titled "The House of Life," Rossetti organized them in a quasi-chronological sequence, thus implying a narrative basis absent in the individual poems.

And this leads to my hypothesis that, as a general rule, Rossetti's initial conceptions take the form of an imagined effect rather than an imagined action. Even when the "story" is worked out prior to the poem, as in the case of his fragment "The Orchard-Pit," the initial form of the poetic version is uncertain of its narrative coordinates. Rossetti's revisions are not aimed at transforming emotion into narrative; rather, they use narrative or quasi-narrative detail to ground and thereby intensify emotional content. In this respect, his practice as a poet acknowledged the difference between poetry and painting—although even in Rossetti's work as an artist, ungrounded affect sometimes cries out for a narrative supplement. When William Morris wrote poems on Rossetti paintings like "The Blue Closet" and "Tune of the Seven Towers," he was not translating the subject from one representative mode to another: he was supplying narrative details without which the paintings remain hauntingly inconclusive.

The instance of Morris should remind us that Rossetti was not the only Pre-Raphaelite artist—I use the term *Pre-Raphaelite* in an extended sense—who was also a writer. In their habits of revision, few poets could be more opposed than Rossetti and Morris. While Rossetti labored endlessly over the minutiae of a text, Morris, in contrast, hated dwelling on details and preferred to rewrite a long narrative poem from scratch rather than enter into the "maze of re-writing."[10] While Rossetti agonized over the fine points of punctuation, Morris left them to the printer. While Rossetti sought the approval of his friends—witness his letter to Hall Caine—Morris worked largely in isolation.

These differences do not, however, argue against my view that the practice of art may influence the practice of poetry, for Morris was also a very different kind of artist from Rossetti. He was inept at representing the human form but successful designing two-dimensional patterns that could repeat themselves endlessly. Unlike the framed space of an oil painting, a chintz or wallpaper could, presumably, go on forever. Granted, Morris's textile designs work within defined spaces. But they are not spaces with rigorous borders. (Indeed, in most cases, hiding the border was a desirable effect.) Order in such forms derives not from the frame that encloses but from strongly marked repetition—literally the "pattern" that provides formal balance and, in its larger sense, is prepared to repeat itself. If Morris experienced revision as a "maze," it may have been because in revising small details he lost sight of the large forms that gave structure to his work. Because he wrote with great speed and fluency—characteristics as legendary as Rossetti's fussiness—he was able to remain aware of overarching narrative patterns as he wrote.

Morris's dislike of piecemeal revision is linked with his suspicion of high art. "That talk of inspiration is sheer nonsense," he declared on one occasion. "There is no such thing: it is a mere matter of craftsmanship." "If a chap can't compose an epic poem while he's weaving tapestry . . . he had better shut up, he'll never do any good at all."[11] But the image of Morris writing verses with one hand and operating a loom with the other suggests more than his unpretentious attitude toward poetry; it also suggests that for Morris verse-writing was an activity akin to the repetitive movements of weaving—or pattern design in general. Since he did not take up weaving until after he had written most of his major poetry (including all of his poetry that could be called "epic"), he cannot have been hyperbolizing his own practice. Even his experience as a wallpaper designer was limited when he began writing long verse narratives in the late 1860s. I cannot, therefore, pretend that there is a causal link between Morris's work as a designer and his manner of writing poetry. But it is clear that his work habits as a poet have much in common with his work habits as a designer, and it seems reasonable to assume that both have their origin in a generalized notion of artistic labor. Moreover, because the years in which he learned how to write long narrative poetry were also the years in which he learned how to design wallpapers and chintzes, there may have been mutual reinforcement between the two activities.

This connection has been used as the basis for accusing

Morris of writing poetry that is merely decorative.[12] A proper response to this accusation would question the pejorative sense of the term "decorative" and connect Morris's intentions as a poet with his notion of the role of the "lesser arts" in an ideal society. For the present, however, it suffices to note that the comparison between composition and pattern design describes a creative process, not the artifact it produces. In themselves, Morris's work habits tell us nothing about the artistic value of his poetry.

The analogy between writing poetry and pattern design does, however, suggest a way in which Morris's work habits may have influenced the form of his verse. Unlike a landscape painter, the weaver cannot dart from one point in his work to another. His pattern is determined prior to the start of its reproduction. His labor is a slow, rhythmic process of accumulation, in which revision is possible only by undoing and starting over again.

In weaving, Morris found a creative experience that replicated his earlier experience of writing poems on traditional and therefore largely predetermined subjects. If he enjoyed the experience of writing such verse, his pleasure seems to have had something to do with the notion of literary composition as an act of repetition—his belief that, even in his most original narratives, he was in some sense retelling a story. So conceived, all writing is thus a form of revision. Working with this conception of the creative process, he could take large-scale structure for granted and concentrate instead on embellishment and amplification. Unlike Rossetti, Morris starts out with narrative and supplements it with affect. When he revises a traditional story—as he does when he transforms the *Lax æ la Saga* into "The Lovers of Gudrun" or explores the feelings of Guenevere at a particular moment in Arthurian history—he opens chronological narrative to the representation of emotional states, in effect, subverting the linear thrust of narration by replacing action with psychology. When he repeats basic narrative configurations, as he does in the sequence of *The Earthly Paradise* and in his later prose romances, his purpose would appear to be a rethinking of the emotional life of his characters.

It is easy to emphasize the obvious differences between Rossetti and Morris. In at least one respect, however, the two poets are unexpectedly similar. For both, revision is a matter less of bringing an initial conception to completion than of transforming one kind of artistic conception into another. Revision, for both poets is, in Yeats's terms, an antithetical activity: the quest for an artistic modality opposed to the mode of initial conception. The result is a poetry caught between two modalities, at once both and neither. And so Rossetti's and Morris's notion of "writing literature" may account for the difficulties we face in reading Pre-Raphaelite poetry—for the uncertainty of its genre and therefore our own uncertainty as to how it is to be read.

NOTES

1. David G. Riede, *Dante Gabriel Rossetti and the Limits of Victorian Vision* (Ithaca, N.Y.: Cornell University Press, 1983).

2. Quoted in Janet Camp Troxell, *Rossetti's "Sister Helen"* (New Haven, Conn.: Yale University Press, 1939), p. 13.

3. Ibid.

4. Paull Franklin Baum, ed. *The Blessed Damozel: The Unpublished Manuscript Texts and Collation* (Chapel Hill: University of North Carolina Press, 1937), p. xiv.

5. Robert N. Keane, "D.G. Rossetti's *Poems*, 1870: A Study in Craftsmanship," *Princeton University Library Chronicle* 33 (Spring 1972): 193.

6. David Sonstroem, review of "Essays on the Rossettis," by Robert S. Fraser, ed., *Victorian Poetry* 11 (1973): 83.

7. Joseph H. Gardner, "Rossetti as Wordsmith: The 'Newborn Death' Sonnets of *The House of Life*," *Victorian Poetry* 20 (Autumn–Winter 1982): 27.

8. John Keats, *Letters*, ed. Hyder Edward Rollins, 2 vols. (Cambridge: Harvard University Press, 1958), 1:323.

9. Riede, p. 23.

10. William Morris, *The Collected Letters*, ed. Norman Kelvin, 3 vols. (in progress) (Princeton, N.J.: Princeton University Press, 1984–), 1:155.

11. Quoted in J. W. Mackail, *The Life of William Morris*, (1899; reprint, New York: Benjamin Blom, 1968), 1:186.

12. Philip Henderson, *William Morris: His Life, Work and Friends* (New York: McGraw-Hill, 1967), p. 87; Paul Thompson, *The Work of William Morris* (New York: Viking Press, 1967), p. 170.

4

Retrieving Beatrix Potter's Revision Process

Catherine Golden

Beatrix Potter created a series of twenty-three picture books beginning with her best-known story, *The Tale of Peter Rabbit* (1902). The final versions demonstrate her ability to write cohesive narratives and to draw and paint skillful, naturalist illustrations. However, the manuscripts of these tales allow us to retrieve how Potter envisioned and revised her art and writing. Composing across the sister arts,[1] Potter used a rigorous strategy for textual and graphic revision originally instilled by her Victorian publishers and increasingly by her own, often opposing, impulses. Devising techniques in response to such external and internal sources for revision, she made numerous stylistic and graphic changes. The result is a distinctive repertoire of revision strategies demonstrating Potter's abilities as a reviser in two art forms and the recursive nature of her revision and composition processes.

Writing for *Horn Book* twenty-eight years after the completion of her first and most famous tale, Potter described her revising process: "My usual way of writing is to scribble, and cut out, and write it again and again. The shorter and plainer the better."[2] Although her comment does not reflect the scope of her practices, this is Potter's only existing remark on how she revised. A comparison of *Peter Rabbit* printed privately by Potter in 1901 with the second version published by Frederick Warne & Co. in 1902[3] shows that she "cut" illustrations and "shortened" the narrative to establish the integrity of her first tale. But the manuscripts for this and other tales as well as her correspondence with Warne reveal that what she claims as her own approach to revision—while by no means a complete description of her revising process—is the specific counsel which her lifelong publisher gave her to improve *Peter Rabbit* and subsequent tales.

Peter Rabbit demonstrates Potter's willingness to follow suggestions and restrictions from Warne to ensure her first book's commercial publication. Without actually directing her revisions, they guided them. The manuscript version contains abundant editorial comments from Warne. To make a practical layout for *Peter Rabbit,* Warne advised that Potter trim her text and illustrations. For instance, they suggested that "the book would best be cut down to 32 pictures only."[4] They marked with an *E* possible passages and drawings for "excision," which could be omitted without interfering with the story line. However, they left the actual decisions up to Potter. Complying with their suggestions and restrictions, she combined the text from several pages and cut numerous passages. The appropriateness of Warne's comments can be seen in Potter's agreement to delete a lengthy and rather anticlimactic episode describing how Peter Rabbit's mother earned her livelihood. The writing of this section is uneven; after describing how Mrs. Rabbit knitted mittens, Potter intruded into the narrative to claim "I once bought a pair at a bazaar."[5] Potter had originally placed this six-page sequence between Peter's narrow escape from Mr. McGregor's garden and his punishment with a bitter dose of camomile tea. Potter's deletion of this irrelevant sequence sustains the focus and pace of the short tale.

In their correspondence, Warne also told Potter bluntly that "to make the book a success it is absolutely necessary that the book should be coloured throughout."[6] Potter had chosen not to color the pictures in her own version only in part because of the expense; she thought that the colors of "rabbit brown and green" were "uninteresting."[7] Accepting the opportunity to redo her pictures, she turned her pen-and-ink drawings into color illustrations which engage the viewer, much as Frederick Warne & Co. had predicted. Her use of color in these and other illustrations reveals her skill for precise detail and her early training as a naturalist of flora, fauna, fungi, and landscape.[8]

The margins of the manuscripts of tales following *Peter Rabbit* including *The Tailor of Gloucestor* (1902), *Two Bad Mice* (1904), and *Mrs. Tiggy-Winkle* (1905) contain editorial comments for revision written by Potter as well as to Potter. These manuscripts record an ongoing dialogue between Potter and Norman Warne, the youngest member of the family-run publishing house. From 1902 to 1905 Norman Warne nurtured Potter's talent as an author-illustrator. Their exchanges demonstrate that Norman Warne's critical judgment was often better than Potter's own. He particularly instilled Potter's practice of cutting and her conception of revision as deletion. Before submitting The *Tailor of Gloucestor* to Warne, Potter printed her second book privately, including in it many popular rhymes and riddles. One lengthy section which again interrupted the plot contained most of these rhymes; minor characters sing rhymes for several pages, such as "Little Poll Parrot / Sat in a garret / Eating toast and tea! / A little brown mouse / Jumped into the house, / And stole it all away."[9] Norman Warne marked these sections with an *E*, suggesting their intrusion and irrelevance. Potter had anticipated his response. In a letter she told Norman Warne: "I was quite sure in advance you would cut out . . . all my favorite rhymes! Which was one of the reasons why I printed it myself."[10] Reducing the number of rhymes from twenty-two in the privately printed version to six in Warne's version, Potter came to accept Norman Warne's judgment. Public opinion also concurred. The greater popularity of Warne's *Tailor of Gloucestor* (1902) persuaded Potter to prune routinely and to rely more on her own writing for subsequent narratives.

Potter was still including irrelevant rhymes and intrusive narrative sections in her manuscripts at the time of Norman Warne's death in 1905.[11] Having assimilated Norman Warne's approach to revision as deletion, however, she wrote alongside these sections: "Leave out some," "Shorten this page," and "Cut."[12] In revising she deleted rhymes, tightened lengthy passages, and improved her wording. Before submitting her manuscripts to the publishing house, she wrote certain sentences "again and again," much as she described in her *Horn Book* article, and often changed individual words and sentences after trying out her manuscripts on various children she knew. Even after Warne accepted her text, she often continued to propose sentence-level revisions of the galley proofs right up to the point of publication. For example, in the manuscript for *Mr. Jeremy Fisher* (1906) she lightly crossed out her initial word choice of "tethered" in a description of Jeremy's boat—"It was tethered to a water plant in the middle of the pond"—and substituted "moored" in its place. For the final text, she further simplified her diction by changing this word to "tied."[13]

While Potter had seemingly adapted the principles behind Warne's recommendations to revise, she independently devised inventive revision techniques to employ Warne's suggestions as well as to satisfy her own personal preferences. Although she continued to rewrite passages "again and again," her manuscripts reveal an elaborate and systematic revision practice in her art as well as her writing which points out the incompleteness of her revision process espoused in *Horn Book*.

To guide her graphic revisions when preparing her book illustrations, Potter frequently wrote notes to herself within her sketches to instruct her revisions.[14] Distinct from the narrative, these linguistic cues helped her achieve correspondence between text and illustration (for which she is renowned),[15] highlight theme, develop character, and, most importantly, plan additional graphic revisions which she made when replacing these notes with artistic details. For example, in the sketch illustrating the line from *Benjamin Bunny*, "Then [Benjamin] suggested that they should fill the pocket handkerchief with onions, as a little present for his Aunt" (p. 30), Potter labeled the roughly drawn outlines "Peter," "Benjamin," "onions," and "handkerchief." She also wrote more extensively toward the bottom of the sketch: "The handkerchief will make a good bit of colour all through the book." Employing the future tense, this note suggests that Potter did not originally perceive the importance of color until she was in the process of revising the tale. The symbolic potential of the red handkerchief may also have been realized at this point. As a result of this insight, she added the meaning-laden detail to a significant number of illustrations. In the final version sixteen of the twenty-six predominately "rabbit brown and green" illustrations contain the colorful red handkerchief, which becomes a recurring visual motif of Peter's shame.

To facilitate her textual and graphic revision, Potter devised a technique of superimposition akin to modern collage which allowed her to improve but retain rather than discard material cut during revision. The superimposition technique in graphic and textual revision emphasizes the recursive nature of Potter's revision process. To facilitate textual superimposition she prepared thin strips of paper which she pasted over parts of the text in order to write out word- and sentence-level revisions suggested by Warne and increasingly by herself. Potter's habit of preparing these strips in advance demonstrates the conscious nature of her textual superimposition technique. Like her other manuscripts, *Tom Kitten* (1907) contains extra blank strips to accommodate additional, anticipated textual amendments. The manuscript also shows how Potter improved her wording. She carefully pasted, for example, the shorter, colloquial sentences "Now keep your frocks clean, children! You must walk on your hind legs" over the more cumbersome sentence "Now my children you must walk on your hind legs to keep your clothes on."[16]

Potter also adapted her technique of superimposition for graphic revision to compensate for her inability to draw human figures. Warne was critical of her human figures and frequently sent back those with human representation to be redrawn [17]; in one such illustration returned for *Peter Rabbit* what Warne perceived as Mr. McGregor's nose was intended as his ear. Potter freely admitted in a letter to Warne that she "never learnt to draw figures, but it is very much more satisfactory to have another try at them and I am very glad you have sent them back."[18] However, treating illustration as collage, she did not eliminate and reattempt such unsatisfactory illustrations. Rather than "have another try at them" entirely, she returned to her original, unsuccessful illustrations and built upon them to improve them. For *Mrs. Tiggy-Winkle,* instead of redoing the illustrations of Lucie's head, her one human representation, Potter sketched Lucie's head on separate sheets of paper many times until she finally achieved a series of identical, more accurate human faces. Then she returned to her initial compositions and pasted the improved heads over the original, unsuccessful ones.[19]

Potter's revision technique of graphic superimposition allowed her to improve her images. Equally important, it enabled her to retain her materials. Retrieval, another of Potter's revision techniques, also enabled her to retain graphic and textual materials which she apparently cut only reluctantly during her revision process. Actually, Potter rarely discarded material which she deleted while revising but rather used her literary and visual deletions as a composing source out of which she created new tales. For example, she never did abandon the text and illustrations which she cut from *Peter Rabbit* (1902) at Warne's suggestion. Possessive of the story line, characters, and visual art of the privately printed *Peter Rabbit* (1901), Potter seems to have consciously reshuffled these cards in her deck of material for storybooks. Pictures and passages dropped from the privately printed version of *Peter Rabbit* for Warne's version are revived in tales including *Benjamin Bunny* (1904), *Flopsy Bunnies* (1909), and *Mr. Tod* (1912), all of which re-create and build upon the first adventure of Peter Rabbit.

The interconnectedness of her revision and composition processes suggests that Potter was able to revise through deletion with the security of knowing she could retrieve these original materials for new compositions. As she composed recursively, Potter did not simply recycle materials discarded during a previous revision. In its new context, each retrieved illustration or passage functions literally as a re-vision. Using a method akin to her technique of graphic superimposition as collage, Potter frequently added new details to existing illustrations to cast them anew. In addition, she also retrieved and recontextualized a consistent cast of characters—Peter Rabbit, Mrs. Rabbit, Peter's sisters, Benjamin Bunny, Mr. and Mrs. McGregor, and Old Mr. Benjamin Bunny.

Unlike her second and third tales, Potter's fourth story, *The Tale of Benjamin Bunny,* is another rabbit tale. The story describes how with the aid of his cousin, Benjamin, Peter rescues his clothes from Mr. McGregor's garden, outsmarts Mr. McGregor, and redeems himself in the eyes of his hardworking mother. Margaret Lane has aptly called the story "a true sequel to *Peter Rabbit.*"[20] In addition to continuing the first tale, the fourth story contains passages and illustrations which Potter deleted from it to ensure her first book's publication by Warne. Once Potter securely established herself with Warne, she retrieved nearly the entire six-page sequence on Mrs. Rabbit's livelihood. While the domestic sequence interrupts the adventure of *Peter Rabbit,* it acts as a theme for the sustained domestic plot of *Benjamin Bunny.*

Benjamin Bunny exemplifies Potter's method of retrieving her materials deleted while revising a previous tale. Potter revived the narrative section about Mrs. Rabbit nearly verbatim. On the third page of the story she writes that Mrs. Rabbit, a widow, "earned her livelihood by knitting rabbit-wool mittens and muffettees (I once bought a pair at a bazaar). She also sold herbs, and rosemary, tea, and rabbit tobacco (which is what *we* call lavender)" (p. 13). In this new context the description of Mrs. Rabbit's occupation allows us to sympathize with her predicament. The widow fears that she will have to work even harder knitting and selling her wares to buy new clothes for her wayward son. Unfortunately, Potter retrieved her favorite, previously cut material unselectively. Although softened by its placement in a parentheses, the authorial intrusion works to the detriment of *Benjamin Bunny.* The pronoun "we," emphasized through italics, conflates and confuses the narrator's world with the fanciful animal world inside the narrative frame.

The frontispiece for *Benjamin Bunny* establishes an immediate connection between the first, unrevised version of *Peter Rabbit* and *Benjamin Bunny.* The colored frontispiece of Mrs. Rabbit selling tea and tobacco is actually a revision of a pen-and-ink drawing deleted from the privately printed *Peter Rabbit* for Warne's version. Mrs. Rabbit appears equally domestic and industrious in the frontispiece for *Benjamin Bunny*, which introduces the important theme of Mrs. Rabbit's livelihood even before the tale begins. In the original illustration, which appears in *Peter Rabbit* (1901), Mrs. Rabbit is making bunches of lavender. In the revision, which appears in *Benjamin Bunny*, Mrs. Rabbit is knitting, much as she is in another illustration cut from the first version of *Peter Rabbit*. Although this change of occupation is a minor one, it shows Potter's desire to retain at least a part of every illustration dropped during her revision of her first tale. In revising the image, Potter also shifted Mrs. Rabbit's placement and repositioned the four, small rabbits, but she maintained their arrangement and again set the siblings apart according to their gender. In both versions of the illustration the three nearly identical rabbit sisters are in full view bathed in light. Peter, however, is only partially visible in the shadows of the fir tree knoll. Placing Peter in semidarkness in *Benjamin Bunny* underscores his waywardness and visually foreshadows how his adventurous nature will lead him on another journey into Mr. McGregor's garden. The revision also contains more vivid detail. Potter added to the frontispiece a sign reading "Josephine Rabbit licensed to sell TEA & TOBACCO" and a table which displays foods to be sold in her shop. Mrs. Rabbit's clothes, her shop, and the facial expressions of all the rabbits are more clearly defined, and pastel colors and shading are added to the entire plate.

Another deleted illustration reappearing with minor changes in *Benjamin Bunny* features Benjamin's father smoking a pipe of rabbit tobacco.[21] This illustration speaks eloquently to Potter's process of retrieving and so retaining the deletions from her revising process. Employing her strategy of writing linguistic cues in her sketches to guide graphic revision, Potter wrote in her manuscript underneath a rough sketch of a rabbit in a frock coat: "The old rabbit you left out of the first book." Potter's note refers her to a sketch of a buck rabbit carrying a switch and smoking a pipe of Mrs. Rabbit's home-cured tobacco also cut from the privately printed *Peter Rabbit* for Warne's version. The deleted image is allowed to carry far more meaning in *Benjamin Bunny.* The anonymous buck rabbit becomes Benjamin's father, a heroic but stern character who reprimands Peter and Benjamin with the switch he holds in both illustrations.

The graphic revisions of the cover page of *The Tale of Benjamin Bunny* attest to Potter's difficulty in letting go of her original story line of *Peter Rabbit* and the problems that arise when new compositions are born of materials deleted from earlier texts. In the cover design of the manuscript, Potter included two rabbits, one with "Peter?" written beside it. His outline is lightly crossed out. Given Peter's role in the story that reveals his fate, his inclusion in the final cover design would have been appropriate. The final design, however, features Benjamin alone. Wearing a brown jacket and his trademark green tamoshanter, Benjamin carries the red handkerchief, a symbol referring only tangentially to Peter because it temporarily clothed him. Although Potter revised the cover design to increase Benjamin's status, ironically her textual revisions diminish his importance and increase Peter's status. In the manuscript, she crossed out, for example, an important clause providing Benjamin's personal motivation for entering Mr. McGregor's garden.[22] Benjamin becomes only a minor character in the tale bearing his name, but he assumes the lead on its cover; such revisions created an imbalance between her verbal and visual characterizations of Benjamin in the final version of *Benjamin Bunny.* The revised text of *Benjamin Bunny* and the cover design of the manuscript allow us to retrieve Potter's overt preference for her first storybook hero and her desire to continue Peter's garden adventure in the form of a different tale.

In time Potter's personal preference to keep what she cut while revising shaped the form of numerous tales following *Benjamin Bunny.* Her practice of retrieving the deletions from her first story extended to favorite materials which she retained in Warne's *Peter Rabbit* (1902) as well as to other literary and visual sources. From her "picture letters" to children,[23] as she called her illustrated correspondence, she retrieved ideas for additional tales, including *Two Bad Mice* (1904) and *Little Pig Robinson* (1930). From her sketchbooks of naturalist drawings she retrieved models of rabbits, mice, and barnyard animals in lake, wood, and garden settings to guide her creation of naturalist illustrations for tales, such as *Jemima Puddle-Duck* (1908) and *Mrs. Tittlemouse* (1910).[24] From *Peter Rabbit* and *Benjamin Bunny* she retrieved and developed her favorite story lines, characters, and visual art in the text and illustrations of a number of new tales.[25] Potter recontextualized and sustained the feud between Mr. McGregor and the rabbits inhabiting her storybook world in *Flopsy Bunnies*. In *Flopsy Bunnies* and again in *Mr. Tod* she recalled her familiar cast of favorite characters—Peter, Benjamin, Old Benjamin Bunny, Flopsy, and Mrs. Rabbit—and aged them to allow their lives to mirror societal conventions. As Leslie Linder notes, "Peter has a life-story."[26] And the "life-story" exists because of Beatrix Potter's recursive composition process which grew from the text and illustrations she cut but retained while revising *The Tale of Peter Rabbit* (1902).

NOTES

1. Potter was one of a distinctive group of Victorian author-illustrators which includes Lewis Carroll, George Du Maurier, Kate Greenaway, Rudyard Kipling, Edward Lear, Dante Gabriel Rossetti, and William Thackeray. All references to Beatrix Potter's works are from *The World of Peter Rabbit: The Original and Authorized Editions* (London: Frederick Warne, 1987).

2. Beatrix Potter, "'Roots' of the Peter Rabbit Tales," *Horn Book* 5.2 (1929): 72.

3. The first version of *The Tale of Peter Rabbit* was based on an illustrated letter written to the son of her former governess on September 4, 1893. She deleted the salutation to "Dear Noel," expanded the text, and added forty-two pen-and-ink illustrations and a colored frontispiece. The tale in this form was rejected by at least six publishers including Warne. Determined to see her tale published, Potter printed it privately. The 1901 version met with a considerable degree of success among a financially privileged circle (prominent figures such as Sir Arthur Conan Doyle bought it for their children). A facsimile of "The Peter Rabbit Letter" with commentary by Linder appears in Leslie Linder, *A History of the Writings of Beatrix Potter* (London: Frederick Warne, 1978), pp. 7–14.

4. Quoted in Linder, *History*, p. 95.

5. Ibid., p. 57.

6. Ibid., p. 95.

7. Ibid.

8. In the late nineteenth century when Potter entered the field of children's

writing and illustration, both literary and artistic professions were commonly pursued by women. She became an author-illustrator when the exclusively male scientific community at Kew Gardens barred her from her chosen artistic career as a naturalist artist. For a complete discussion of Potter's training and aspiration to be a naturalist of flora, fauna, fungi, and landscape, see Catherine Golden, "Beatrix Potter: Naturalist Artist," *Woman's Art Journal* 11.1 (1990): 16–20. For Potter's naturalist art, see Linder's *The Art of Beatrix Potter* (London: Frederick Warne, 1971), Anne Stevenson Hobbs and Joyce Irene Whalley's *Beatrix Potter: The V & A Collection: The Leslie Linder Bequest of Beatrix Potter Material* (London: Victoria and Albert Museum and Frederick Warne, 1985); and Anne Stevenson Hobbs' *Beatrix Potter's Art* (London: Frederick Warne, 1989).

9. Linder, *History*, p. 130.

10. Quoted in Margaret Lane, *The Magic Years of Beatrix Potter* (London: Frederick Warne, 1978), p. 105.

11. As Potter's association with Warne continued from 1902, her almost daily correspondence came to be handled almost exclusively by Norman Warne. The editorial attention which she received may be due in part to her personal relationship with Norman. His romantic interest in Beatrix seemingly developed through their discussions of her work (Lane, p. 121). They were engaged in 1905 just after Potter completed her fifth tale, *Two Bad Mice* (1904); Norman Warne died suddenly, one month after their engagement. For more information on Norman Warne and his personal relationship with Potter, see the biographies of Lane and Taylor.

12. These notes appear in the unpaginated manuscript of "The Tale of Mrs. Tiggy-Winkle," contained in the Potter Archives, part of The Lake District National Trust, Ambleside, England.

13. A photograph of a page of the manuscript from *Jeremy Fisher* showing Potter's word-level substitution is reprinted in Judy Taylor's recent biography *Beatrix Potter: Artist, Storyteller, and Countrywoman* (London: Frederick Warne, 1985), p. 105.

14. These notes can be found in the sketches of numerous manuscripts contained in the Potter Archives. These include "The Tailor of Gloucestor," "The Tale of the Pie and the Patty-pan," "The Tale of Benjamin Bunny," and "The Tale of Two Bad Mice." In *History*, Linder also comments upon Potter's technique of writing notes in her sketches of "Benjamin Bunny," p. 145.

15. There were a few exceptions. In *The Tale of the Pie and the Patty-pan* (1905) Potter wrote in the narrative that Ribby's butter dish is blue and white and that Ribby the cat does not actually bake her pie. She painted the butter dish pink and white and apparently made the pie a darker shade than the white of uncooked pastry. Lane (p. 136) suggests that the discrepancy between text and picture of the pie may be due to the printing; the pastry in the original illustration is the color of ivory.

16. Unpaginated, the manuscript version of *Tom Kitten* is part of the Potter Archives. This same method of textual revision appears in other manuscripts also contained in the Potter Archives including "The Tailor of Gloucestor,"

"The Tale of Benjamin Bunny," "The Tale of Mrs. Tiggy-Winkle," "The Tale of Two Bad Mice," and "The Tale of the Pie and the Patty-pan." Following Potter's move to the Lake District in 1905, she made many textual changes in response to the reactions of audiences of children she assembled in the town of Sawrey to preview her manuscripts. The manuscripts all contain extra strips of paper which Potter tucked between the pages in anticipation of additional textual amendments.

17. The illustration of "Mrs. McGregor and the Rabbit Pie" was of great concern to Warne because of the way Potter drew her face as a caricature. An old and sour-faced woman clutching a pie decorated with a rabbit's tail shows the consequences of a rabbit adventuring in a farmer's garden and intensifies the realism of the tale. Unfortunately, this picture was never used in the Warne version because the publishers did not like the old woman's face. Potter revised the image of Mrs. McGregor, presumably making it a self-portrait, but this change did not satisfy Warne either. Warne removed the revised illustration after the fourth printing. Although this illustration is of an undeniably lesser quality than her illustrations of flora and fauna, her publisher's deletion of this compelling illustration made Warne's *Peter Rabbit* more fanciful than the privately printed version.

18. Quoted in Linder, *History*, p. 103.

19. In *The Art of Beatrix Potter* Linder includes a sketch of "Lucie and the Little Door in the Back of the Hill," p. 310. The sketch contains six "tries" at drawing Lucie's head (in profile, full view, and three-quarter view) and four "tries" at drawing her ankle and foot (also in different positions). Close examination of the original watercolor illustrations for *Tiggy-Winkle* (contained in the Potter Archives) reveals Potter's method of carefully pasting improved heads over her earlier, unsuccessful attempts.

20. Lane, p. 117.

21. For the revised illustration appearing in *Benjamin Bunny*, Potter dropped the rabbit's hat and pocket watch and modified its coat by removing the three buttons. She also changed the length and angle of the pipe, enlarged the rabbit's fluffy tail, and embellished the setting by situating the rabbit on a stone wall alongside a pear tree.

22. The deleted clause explained that Mrs. Rabbit, Benjamin's aunt, had caught him smoking rabbit tobacco the day before. This deleted clause also suggests why, once in the garden, Benjamin insists that he and his cousin "fill the pocket handkerchief with onions, as a little present for his Aunt" (p. 30).

23. Quoted in Linder, ed. *The Journal of Beatrix Potter from 1881 to 1897* (London: Frederick Warne, 1979), p. 250.

24. Potter's picture letters originated as a way to amuse the children of former governess Annie Carter Moore. She wrote illustrated letters principally to the four older Moore children—Noel, Eric, Frida, and Norah Moore—containing stories loosely based on her travels. *Peter Rabbit* was the first illustrated letter she turned into a story. She returned to many picture letters and retrieved ideas for characters, plot, and her visual art; see, for example, "The Little Pig Robinson

Letter" (March 28, 1894), "The Winchelsea Letter" (January 26, 1900)—basis for *Two Bad Mice,* and "The Squirrel Nutkin Letter" (September 25, 1901) in Linder, *History,* pp. 15–17, 38–41, 54–69. Examples of Potter's naturalist drawings informing her book illustrations can be seen in "Gardens, Plant Studies, and Still Lifes" and "Animal Studies" in Linder's *The Art of Beatrix Potter* and "Early Work," "Natural History," and "Backgrounds For Books," in Hobbs and Whalley's *Beatrix Potter: The V & A Collection.* The section entitled "Backgrounds for Books," though particularly useful, mixes rough drafts of book illustrations with naturalist drawings, only the latter of which are part of Potter's visual source of material for retrieval. Desiring accuracy, the authors have placed in this section only those drawings "whose relevance to a particular work was immediately obvious" (72). However, in a personal letter to the author, 7 October 1987, Hobbs confirms that Potter's principle for retrieval operates on a much larger scale than suggested in "Backgrounds for Books," and further adds that since the book's publication she also has discovered direct connections between materials placed within "Early Work" and "Natural History" and Potter's book illustrations. For further discussion of the connection between Potter's naturalist studies and book illustrations, see Golden's "Beatrix Potter: Naturalist Artist."

25. For *Mrs. Tiggy-Winkle* Potter revived only the familiar costumes of her favorite characters, such as Peter's blue jacket, Squirrel Nutkin's red tail-coat, and Mrs. Rabbit's red handkerchief, which temporarily clothed wayward Peter. *Appley Dapply's Nursery Rhymes* (1917) is another tale which builds upon the initial adventures of *Peter Rabbit*; it contains Cotton-tail's courtship in verse. In *The Tale of Ginger and Pickles* (1909) many of Potter's characters are reintroduced as customers in the shop managed by Ginger the cat and Pickles the terrier. Wearing his blue jacket, Peter Rabbit reappears in these illustrations. Potter also introduces other familiar characters including Mr. Jeremy Fisher, Mrs. Tiggy-Winkle, Jemima Puddle-Duck, Squirrel Nutkin, and Tom Kitten.

26. Linder, ed. *The History of The Tale of Peter Rabbit* (London: Frederick Warne, 1976), p. 61.

5

"It is myself that I remake": W. B. Yeats's Revisions to His Early Canon

George Bornstein

For the 1908 eight-volume edition of *The Collected Works in Verse and Prose of William Butler Yeats* the forty-three-year-old author composed the following quatrain in explanation of his lifelong habit of poetic revision:

> The friends that have it I do wrong
> When ever I remake a song,
> Should know what issue is at stake:
> It is myself that I remake.[1]

Those lines boldly extend the subject of revision from the poem itself to the persona of the poet, whose construction preoccupied Yeats throughout his career. Scholars have been quick to understand the importance of Yeats's revisions to individual poems, now easily accessible in the *Variorum* edition, but slower to track the significance of his recasting of larger units of his verse.[2] Similarly, Yeatsians have for a long time appreciated the truth of

Hugh Kenner's contention that Yeats "didn't accumulate poems, he wrote books. . . . And the unit in which to inspect and discuss his development is not the poem or sequence of poems but the volume," but have largely neglected his subsequent revision of those volumes, particularly the early ones.[3] I should like to suggest here that Yeats's revision of his early poetry, and consequently of his early poetic self, involves not simply his stylistic revisions to individual poems but rather a complex and deliberate reworking of the larger divisions into which he organized his work. Each successive unit from *The Wanderings of Oisin and Other Poems* (1889) through *The Countess Kathleen and Various Legends and Lyrics* (1892) to the first collected *Poems* (1895) marks a careful construction both of a canon and of an appropriate poetic self. Understanding Yeats's maneuvers during those years will enable us at the end to consider the implications of the two separate orderings in which the entire body of his poetry is currently available to readers, and the relevance of such study for the current gap in our profession between sophisticated textual scholarship on the one hand and advanced critical theory on the other.

The ordering of a volume into a unit, so familiar to students of Yeats's later poetry, attracted him from the first. Although poets from Dante (in the *Vita Nuova*) and Petrarch (in the *Canzoniere*) had sought to arrange their shorter poems into coherent and meaningful sequences, that tendency became particularly prevalent in the English line running through Spenser and Milton to the great Romantics.[4] That was precisely the tradition in which Yeats saw himself, of course, and he studied its components with care. In the works of his two favorite Romantics, for example, he would have found careful and complex ordering in Blake's *Songs of Innocence and of Experience* or Shelley's *Prometheus Unbound, with Other Poems*.[5] As with his predecessors, both external and internal evidence reveals Yeats's intentions. The principles of selection and ordering appear very early. In January 1888, a year before publication of his first book, he told a correspondent:

> The book will have for longest poem 'The Wanderings of Oisin' . . . an irish poem of some length and about my best.

> The remainder will be made up of short lyrics and ballads—irish a good many of them,—and a few dramatic sketches & a few philosophical quatrains. So far as I see this will be the selection but when I get back to London—I start to morrow—and begin sorting things, I may modify it indefinately [sic].[6]

The selection and sorting mentioned there occupied Yeats for the next several months, and his surviving papers contain various lists for ordering the volume (as they do for the two subsequent ones as well).[7] The internal evidence of the volume itself supports Yeats's intentions, though he succeeded less skillfully and comprehensively than he would in future collections.

The first thing to notice about the order of the thirty-one poems contained in *The Wanderings of Oisin and Other Poems* (1889) is that it is not chronological. (See Figure 5.1.) On the contrary, Yeats finished the opening title poem, "The Wanderings of Oisin," among the last in the collection and the concluding "Island of Statues" among the first. Nor did he arrange the poems between those two chronologically. Instead, he strove for an architectonic order punctuated by the three major pieces in the collection—"Oisin," "Island," and, at the exact middle of the thirty-one poems, "Mosada." The title poem emphasized the Irish component of the volume and began the antinomial vacillation between human and supernatural worlds which permeated the book, as it eventually would all of Yeats's work; moreover, Oisin's alternate attraction first to the Tir na nOg of Niamh and then to the heroic world of the Fenians, combined with a disdain for the contemporary fallen world, sounds the dominant themes of the collection. The volume proceeds through foiled Indian, Arcadian, and Irish questers to its midpoint in the sixteenth poem, where the Moorish enchantress Mosada seeks vainly to use her magical arts to recover her lost lover and eventually commits suicide. The second half of the volume salutes more the fallen human world (even its three fairy poems seem to anthropomorphize their faeries) en route to the concluding "Island of Statues," in which a female quester attains immortality at the price of eventually outliving her mortal lover.

Figure 5.1 From *The Wanderings of Oisin and Other Poems* (1889)

CONTENTS.

The volume thus seems to end where it began, reiterating the initial incompatibilities in a static order at variance with the dynamic deployment of poems in Yeats's mature books. Its unity resulted partly from exclusion rather than inclusion, for two of the six published poems which Yeats chose to omit from the book comprised his most overtly political work to date: "The Two Titans: A Political Poem" with its contemporary relevance and the recently discovered "The Protestants' Leap (Lug-na-Gal, Sligo)" with its historical memory of Cromwellian times.[8]

Yeats's next volume, *The Countess Kathleen and Various Legends and Lyrics* (1892), stands in obvious counterpoint to his first collection. (See Figure 5.2.) Both books carry titles that emphasize their major poems and yet allow for complex patterning in the manner of Wordsworth and Coleridge's *Lyrical Ballads, with a Few Other Poems* (1798), Keats's *Lamia, Isabella, The Eve of St. Agnes, and Other Poems* (1820), or Shelley's *Prometheus Unbound, with Other Poems* (1820).[9] Moreover, the two title poems—one a romance or small epic, the other a poetic drama—interact in complex ways. In his late poem "The Circus Animals' Desertion," Yeats called "The Countess Kathleen" a "counter-truth" (VP 629) to "The Wanderings of Oisin." It is a counter-truth partly through such characteristic Yeatsian dualities as male/female and pagan/Christian, but primarily in that its protagonist errs through excessive concern for social improvement in the fallen everyday world rather than through disdain for it and devotion either to otherworldly attractions or to a legendary past. The remainder of the volume, which Yeats would later reorganize as the "Rose" poems, was arranged not chronologically but instead to present a countertruth to the title poem. In it Yeats moves from "To the Rose upon the Rood of Time" to the concluding "Apologia Addressed to Ireland in the Coming Days" in an implicit argument that his qualified devotion to the Rose of Intellectual Beauty allows him to steer a middle course between Oisin and Kathleen. He thus emerges as a true Irish poet faithful equally to the supernatural and the human spheres. The volume provided a more unified account of the poet-persona's development than did its predecessor, and it changed less when he revised it for future collections.

Figure 5.2 From *The Countess Kathleen and Various Legends and Lyrics* (1892)

Yeats's letters reveal that from the start he intended in the book we know as *Poems* (1895) to remake radically the canon of his work to date and to set a pattern for future volumes. These concerns extended even to physical appearance. As he explained to his publisher T. Fisher Unwin during contract negotiations, "I am very anxious to get out the volume in such a way that I can make all my future books of verse resemble it in size &

printing" (CLI 402). He originally intended to call it not *Poems* but rather *Under the Moon* (CLI 411). That title carried the normal association of sublunary change and the additional Yeatsian one of desire for escape from mortal limits, as in his later remark that "all that is under the moon thirsts to escape out of bounds, to lose itself in some unbounded tidal stream."[10] It also had a special meaning for the projected collection, as a publisher's announcement which Yeats apparently approved made clear: "Old writers were of opinion that the moon governed by her influence peasants, sailors, fishermen, and all obscure persons; and as the symbols of Mr. Yeats's poetry are taken almost wholly from the traditions and manners of the Connaught peasantry, he has selected the title 'Under the Moon' for his forthcoming book" (CLI 411). In the end, though, he settled on the title *Poems,* rejecting *Collected Poems* because that title "would be soon, I hope, made obsolete by my new books of verse" (CLI 434). That resistance to closure continued unabated, and Yeats did not use *Collected Poems* as a title until 1933.

Yeats devoted much of the fall and winter of 1894–95 to rewriting and rearranging his earlier work into a new canon. (See Figure 5.3.) His chief innovation—rearrangment of the lyrics from his first volume into a section called "Crossways" and of those from his second into one called "The Rose"—came relatively late. The projected table of contents he sent to his publisher in November of 1894 begins with the three long works, simply groups the Irish and Rose poems together without subtitle, and concludes with a truncated "Crossways" containing only the Indian and Arcadian ones from the 1889 volume. The final version, of course, begins (after the prefatory poem) with the countertruths of "The Wanderings of Usheen" and "The Countess Cathleen," and proceeds through the appropriately named new verse play "The Land of Heart's Desire" to two sections of poems called "The Rose" (containing lyrics mostly from the 1892 collection) and "Crossways" (containing poems from the 1889 volume). Yeats explained the significance of the headings in his preface to the book:

This book contains all the writer cares to preserve out of his previous volumes of verse. He has revised and to a large extent rewritten. . . . He has printed the ballads and lyrics from the same volume as *The Wanderings of Usheen,* and two ballads written at the same time, though published later, in a section named *Crossways,* because in them he tried many pathways; and those from the same volume as *The Countess Cathleen* in a section named *The Rose*, for in them he has found, he believes, the only pathway whereon he can hope to see with his own eyes the Eternal Rose of Beauty and Peace. (VP 845–46)

Figure 5.3 From *Poems* (1895) (Prefatory Poem: To Some I Have Talked with by the Fire)

The biggest change in the lyrics occurred in "Crossways." All the poems in "The Rose" had appeared together in 1892, although Yeats in 1895 moved two to "Crossways," dropped a third, and rearranged their order. In contrast, he drastically cut the thirty poems (besides the title one) of *The Wanderings of Oisin and Other Poems* to fourteen for "Crossways," which he augmented by "The Ballad of Father O'Hart" and "The Ballad of the Foxhunter." The sixteen poems Yeats dropped from the earlier collection (seventeen if we include "The Island of Statues" II,3, from which he salvaged only the song "The Cloak, the Boat, and the Shoes") tell us a great deal about his new self-image as poet. As the only scholar to consider the matter, Thomas Parkinson has pointed out that Yeats dropped some because their style was so archaic and otherwise distasteful that he lacked skill to rewrite them, others because they seemed inferior or redundant, and still others because their subject matter was either too remote from contemporary Ireland (some of the Indian, Arcadian, or Spanish pieces) or too close to it (like the one on Nettleship's picture at the Royal Hibernian Academy).[11] This last tendency exaggerated further the original exclusion of overtly political verse from the 1889 volume, and Yeats excluded his subsequent poem on Parnell's death "Mourn—and Then Onward!" (1891) this time as well. He emerged as an Irish poet devoted to tradition and rural Ireland, to various aristocracies and to the peasantry, and to esoteric pursuit of ideal Beauty but not to contemporary causes. Not until after the turn of the century would he include overtly political verse in his published collections.

"Crossways" found its final form in 1895, with eight Arcadian or Indian poems neatly balanced by eight following Irish ones. "The Rose," in contrast, continued to vary in contents and arrangement. The biggest change occurred in 1925, when Yeats for the first time printed "Crossways" before "The Rose" and thus restored the chronology between the sections, although the arrangement of poems within each section continued to be on nonchronological principles. Rather than rehearse those changes here or Yeats's vacillating thought about whether collections of his work should begin with "The Wanderings of Oisin," I should like to jump to the present, when readers are offered Yeats's early poems—along with his later ones—in two different orderings and to meditate on some of the implications of those discrete formats.

As contemporary readers, we encounter Yeats's poems in two distinct orders. *The Variorum Edition of the Poems of W. B. Yeats* (Figure 5.4) begins with "The Wanderings of Oisin" followed by "Crossways" and "The Rose" and proceeds through Yeats's canon by interspersing the longer narrative poems chronologically between the various books of lyrics. In contrast, the old *Collected Poems of W. B. Yeats* and its new (1983) replacement, *The Poems: A New Edition* (Figure 5.5), begin with "Crossways" and "The Rose" as the first two divisions of the section called "Lyrical," which includes the major lyrical volumes in chronological order; "The Wanderings of Oisin" appears at the end as the first of the section of longer poems called "Narrative and Dramatic."[12] Both orders have some textual authority behind them. The *Variorum* descends from the two-volume 1949 *Poems*, which itself derives from the never-published Coole Edition (or Edition de Luxe), which Yeats devoted considerable time to preparing in the early 1930s. *Poems: A New Edition* descends from the 1933 *Collected Poems* (as does the later *Collected Poems*), the last published collected version which Yeats approved. To make matters even more complex, Yeats also sanctioned a never-published Scribner edition in the later 1930s, for which he planned to use the 1933 *Collected Poems* arrangement. We thus have two competing orders for the canon, both sanctioned by Yeats himself at various times during the last decade of his life.[13]

The chief difference between the two orderings in terms of the early poems is that one begins with "The Wanderings of Oisin" and proceeds to the lyrics, while the other begins directly with "Crossways" and postpones "Oisin" until the start of section two, following all the lyrics. This makes for considerable difference in interpretation of the collected poems as a whole. In the former case, Yeats's poetic persona first appears as the author of a long Romantic quest poem firmly in Irish tradition and initiating such typical antinomies as pagan / Christian, active / contemplative, supernatural / human, male / female, and the like. In the latter, he appears instead as a conventional shepherd of European pastoral tradition singing an ambivalent lyric with a different set of antinomies featuring word / deed and dream / truth and not reaching specifically Irish subject matter until the ninth poem in the book. Beginning with "Oisin" fits a more synchronic view of the volume as a whole, while beginning with "Crossways" stresses the diachronic progression in which Yeats did not come to specifically Irish subject matter until later.

This survey of successive remakings of the early canon by Yeats (and later by his editors) raises three issues that I should like to enumerate by way of conclusion. First, Yeats's early canon belongs to the class of texts which eludes our customary rule of final authorial intentions. In this case, it is not possible to determine fully what Yeats's final intentions were but only his

Figure 5.4 From *The Variorum Edition of the Poems of W. B. Yeats*, ed. Allt and Alspach

(first sections only of Contents)

The order of the poems is that of the two-volume definitive edition of 1949. The poems are numbered for convenience of reference.

successive intentions at different stages of his career. As Jerome J. McGann has recently written, "My view is that editors cannot follow the guidance of a rule of final authorial intentions in determining the texts they will print because final authorial intention is a deeply problematic concept."[14] Yet, an editor must print something. As McGann also remarks, "For the editor of late modern works especially, the first and crucial problem is not how to discover corruptions, but how to distinguish and finally choose between textual versions."[15] McGann is concerned to discriminate the social foundation of textual choices, in service of his argument for social production as the ground of literary texts. Here, I would like to emphasize that such choices have thematic and aesthetic consequences: the order in which we read Yeats's early canon affects both our interpretation and our appreciation of it. As critics, we need to know enough textual scholarship to be our own editors, rather than to have our critical field irrevocably defined by an editor's prior judgments. And finally, the particular concerns raised by the study of Yeats's early canon offer a bridge over the current abyss between literary theory and textual scholarship, both of

Figure 5.5 From *The Poems: A New Edition*, ed. Finneran (first sections only of Contents)

33.	The Man who dreamed of Faeryland	43
34.	The Dedication to a Book of Stories selected from the Irish Novelists	45
35.	The Lamentation of the Old Pensioner	46
36.	The Ballad of Father Gilligan	46
37.	The Two Trees	48
38.	To Some I have Talked with by the Fire	49
39.	To Ireland in the Coming Times	50

which have grown increasingly sophisticated in increasing ignorance of each other. Such currently fashionable theoretical terms as the "instability of the text," for example, have a literal sense in textual transmission which precedes any deconstruction we may perform on any particular version. Knowledge of the successive formations of Yeats's early canon already deconstructs whatever final order an editor may have chosen to print, just as knowledge of the successive revisions of any particular poem displaces the privileging of the final version to the exclusion of all others. In remaking his poems, Yeats remade himself, as his quatrain on the subject reminds us. In so doing, he offers us today a middle ground between the old fixed, stable author and fixed, stable text on the one hand and the elimination of the author and substitution of endless textual free play on the other. For what Yeats finally created was a process rather than a product, in which a successive remaking of texts and selves substitutes for the fixing of them. As he wrote, remembering Lady Gregory's tales of Finn, "if any ask what music is the sweetest, we can but answer . . . 'what *happens*.'"[16]

NOTES

1. *The Variorum Edition of the Poems of W. B. Yeats*, ed. Peter Allt and Russell K. Alspach (New York: Macmillan, 1966, corrected third printing), p. 770. Hereafter abbreviated as VP.

2. Thomas Parkinson's *W. B. Yeats Self-Critic: A Study of His Early Verse*

(Berkeley and Los Angeles: University of California Press, 1951) seems to me still the best of the numerous discussions of Yeats's poetic revisions.

3. Hugh Kenner, "The Sacred Book of the Arts," in *Yeats: A Collection of Critical Essays*, ed. John Unterecker (Englewood Cliffs, N.J.: Prentice-Hall, 1963), p. 13. Kenner's essay, which applied to work after *Responsibilities* (1914), first appeared in his book *Gnomon* (New York: Ivan Obolensky, 1958). The best recent discussion of volumes as units in Yeats's poetry is Hazard Adams, "Constituting Yeats's Poems as a Book," in *Yeats, An Annual of Critical and Textual Studies*, ed. Richard J. Finneran (Ann Arbor, Mich.: UMI Research Press, 1986), 4:1–16, which interestingly situates Yeats's penchant for arranging volumes to dramatize a persona in terms of our contemporary critical theories. Parkinson, pp. 8–32, provides the only discussion of Yeats's recasting of a large-scale unit of his early work, the 1895 *Poems*.

4. Neil Fraistat offers a splendid overview of this development in chapters one and two of his important *The Poem and the Book: Interpreting Collections of Romantic Poetry* (Chapel Hill: University of North Carolina Press, 1985).

5. Fraistat, chap. 5.

6. John Kell and Eric Donville, eds., *The Collected Letters of W. B. Yeats: Volume I, 1865–1895* (Oxford: Clarendon Press, 1986), p. 44. Hereafter cited as CLI.

7. See National Irish Inventory (SB) MSS for these lists.

8. For the first poem see VP 687 and for the second John Kelly, "Aesthete among the Athletes: Yeats's Contributions to *The Gael,*" in *Yeats: An Annual of Critical and Textual Studies*, ed. Richard J. Finneran (Ithaca, N.Y.: Cornell University Press, 1984), 2:75–143.

9. See Fraistat, p. 25 and passim.

10. W. B. Yeats, *Explorations* (New York: Macmillan, 1962), p. 25.

11. Parkinson, pp. 20–21.

12. *The Collected Poems of W. B. Yeats* (New York: Macmillan, 1956) and *The Poems: A New Edition*, ed. Richard J. Finneran (New York: Macmillan, 1983). In terms of ordering, the Finneran edition is superior in that it prints such later sections as *Last Poems* in the proper sequence; like the *Variorum*, it also contains additional poems excluded from the canon proper in a separate section at the end.

13. For a fuller account of issues raised in this paragraph, see Richard Finneran, *Editing Yeats's Poems* (New York: St. Martin's Press, 1983), chaps. 1, 2. Warwick Gould attacked Finneran's position in his review of *Poems: A New Edition* in *TLS* for 29 June 1984, which engendered several exchanges over the following two months. See, too, Finneran's "The Order of Yeats's Poems," *Irish University Review* 14 (1984): 165–176.

14. Jerome J. McGann, *A Critique of Modern Textual Criticism* (Chicago and London: University of Chicago Press, 1983), p. 68.

15. McGann, p. 57.

16. Yeats, *Explorations*, p. 26 (emphasis mine).

6

The Evolution of Henley's *In Hospital**

Edward H. Cohen

Henley's *In Hospital,* conceived during his ordeal as a patient in the Royal Infirmary of Edinburgh (1873–75), was a poem in process over a period of fifteen years. The work survives in three published versions. The first, "Hospital Outlines," comprises eighteen sonnets printed in the July 1875 *Cornhill Magazine.*[1] The second, thirteen free-verse "Hospital Sketches," appeared in a charity book, *Voluntaries for an East London Hospital,* 1887.[2] And the third, the "In Hospital" sequence of twenty-eight lyrics and an "Envoy," was included in Henley's first collected poems, *A Book of Verses,* 1888.[3] There are also three principal manuscript texts of the poems. 'Cornhill A' is a series of thirteen sonnets in Henley's hand originally copied fair, then corrected by Robert Louis Stevenson, and subsequently revised by Henley. 'Cornhill B' is a sequence of eighteen autograph "sketches" and "portraits" incorporating twelve of the emended

* For permission to print unpublished manuscripts, I am pleased to acknowledge the generosity of the Beinecke Rare Book and Manuscript Library, Yale University; the Henry E. Huntington Library; the Trustees of the National Library of Scotland; and the Pierpont Morgan Library. Research for this essay was supported by a grant from the American Philosophical Society and a fellowship from the Henry E. Huntington Library.

poems from 'Cornhill A' and six additional sonnets; from this text, also corrected by Stevenson, were set the first printer's proofs of the *Cornhill Magazine* version.[4] The third manuscript text, 'Lazarus,' is an aggregation of fourteen autograph drafts and variants; nine are identified by the notation "Lazarus," and four of these were first published in the *Voluntaries* version.[5] Textual evidence—together with documentary evidence of parallels between particular events and particular poems—reveals that Henley composed most of the hospital poems in response to actual occurrences, either during the infirmary period or, immediately thereafter, during his convalescence at Portobello.[6]

Arthur Symons, who recognized the significance both of Henley's hospital episode and of Henley's hospital poems, once observed: "The poet to whom such an experience has come, the man, perhaps, whom such an experience had made a poet, must be accounted singularly fortunate."[7] But when Henley was admitted to the Royal Infirmary, as Joseph Lister's patient, in the summer of 1873, he had little cause for optimism. In his youth he had contracted an arthritic tuberculosis that infected his hands and feet. He had spent half his life in public hospitals and had suffered the amputation of his left foot, and it was in desperation that he placed himself in Lister's care. He had little reason, moreover, to be optimistic about his poetry. Although he had early dedicated himself to a life of letters and—under T. E. Brown's tutelage—had passed the Oxford Local Schools Examination, his formal education had been curtailed by his illness and by the collapse of his father's finances. He had published nothing more than a series of "Bohemian Ballads," weak imitations of Swinburne, in a London comic weekly.[8] Nevertheless, signing the infirmary admissions book, he offered "writer" as his occupation. And he insisted to his friend Harry Nichols, a London coffeehouse keeper: "If I ever write again, it will be something very different from all that I have hitherto done."[9] Imprisoned in a grim surgical ward, immobilized by an iron splint tied to his right leg, he observed minutely the daily drama of hospital life. A little desk was affixed to his bed, and he began to conceive his hospital sequence.

For this essay, I propose to examine the evolution of a single poem, "Vigil," which exists in every text and every version of *In Hospital,* to illustrate both the succession and the tendencies of Henley's processes of revision.

"Vigil" is an important poem because it represents a compromise between the objectivity of the early *Cornhill* sonnets and the subjectivity of the later *Voluntary* lyrics. It was conceived, as "Night Thoughts," midway through Henley's hospital ordeal, when he had begun to experience profound periods of dejection. On May 17, 1874, he wrote to Harry Nichols: "I need not say I am excessively poor. Still less need have I to declare myself excessively dull. If it were not for sounds of feline ecstasy at night . . . I should hardly guess it was May. *I* don't feel like it at all. I have no will to read, & less to write: the songs & sonnets I vent occasionally are almost Baudelairian in their bitter fixity of *ennui.*"[10]

Night ~~Thoughts~~ Sketch

At midnight when all things are hushed & still,
  Save for a resolute sonorous snore,
  Or cries of feline luxury that thrill
The anguished echoes of the corridor;

When the wee point of gas implacable
  Burns sunlike in my fascinated eyes;
When the clock striking seems to toll a knell
  And hot hard lumps along the mattress rise;

                    life that hums
I lie & listen for ~~the world without,~~
  Heard only in my dreams,—a cinder falls,
    The firelight flickers like a hushed regret,
My neighbour groans & turns, then someone calls

                reverberates
  The snore ~~exasperates~~, the night-nurse comes,
    Noiseless & strange:—"Are ye no sleepin' yet?"

Significant in the original text, its title emended to "Night Sketch," is Henley's selection of parallel images ("cries of feline luxury") to express objectively the subjective tone of his letter to

Nichols. As in the other "Hospital Outlines"—sketches of the infirmary milieu and portraits of nurses, physicians, and fellow patients—the poet's presence here is affirmed by the particularity of his surroundings, by the emphasis upon the physical realities of hospital life. Unlike the other *Cornhill* sonnets, however, there is an anticipation in this "Night Sketch" of Henley's increasing self-absorption.

In February 1875 Leslie Stephen came to Edinburgh to lecture at the Philosophical Institute. For years Henley had been submitting "poems of the Swinburne kind" to the *Cornhill*, and Stephen had promised to pay a visit to this "poor contributor."[11] He cheered Henley and encouraged him and introduced him to Robert Louis Stevenson, who could "lend him books, read his MSS., and be otherwise useful."[12] Indeed, Stevenson did read Henley's manuscripts. "I have a poet in stock here," he wrote to his cousin Bob, "a poor arse in the hospital with one leg off and the other more than shaky. He makes . . . good songs and here and there has a good idea. His hospital sonnets are very true and baldly real—not realistic, a word I have now learned to hate."[13] The text of the poems that Stevenson first read was 'Cornhill A' and on the manuscript of "Night Sketch" he penciled: "Good man! That's what I *do* call realism, and yet like."

Stevenson encouraged Henley to submit the hospital sonnets to the *Cornhill*, and by March 1875 Henley had prepared a second text, 'Cornhill B.' "You have taken great interest in the series," he wrote to Stevenson on March 14, "and I really want your pencil-marks. I shall not ask you to write about them. Pencil the MS as you are wont to do, and post it to me as quickly as you can."[14] In the 'Cornhill A' text, "Night Sketch" was originally titled "Night Thoughts." Revised, the poem in 'Cornhill B' becomes "Night-Picture."

Night-Picture

were
All things ~~are~~ patiently, supremely still
Save for the resolute sonorous snore.

Feline ejaculations rend & thrill
 The flying echoes of the corridor.

O the wee point of gas!—implacable,
 Sunlike it fills my fascinated eyes.
The bedclothes are perverse with life & will.
 And oh! the rocks that in the mattress rise.

Waking I dream: the old time stirs & hums,
 Hushed, in my reverie; a cinder drops;
  The shadow pulses as the loud flames fret;
 My neighbour groans & turns; the snoarer stops,
Chokes, gasps him free again; the nightnurse comes,
  Noiseless & strange:—"Are ye no sleepin' yet?"

This progression is characteristic of Henley's early preoccupation with objectivity in the hospital poems. Even in this most personal of the *Cornhill* sonnets, the poet's involvement is minimized. He is passive. And his presence is affirmed by the sensory intrusions of "feline ejaculations," of his groaning and snoring neighbors, and of the night nurse on her rounds. Stevenson corrected the "sketches" and "portraits," and Henley sent them off to the *Cornhill.*

On April 15, 1875—two days before his discharge from the Royal Infirmary—Henley wrote to Stevenson: "You were a true prophet! The Sonnets have been accepted. . . . I shall want your help over the proofs, & I fancy I shall have either to omit one or two types, which I am unwilling to do, or to introduce one or two fresh ones, which I am anxious to do. If you should see the able-Editor ere you quit the smoke, be so good as to mention this to him, & if he is restive, ease him."[15] The original proof of the *Cornhill* "Hospital Outlines" was printed from the 'Cornhill B' manuscript. Three sets of corrected proofs (several copies of which exist) reveal that Leslie Stephen was indeed "restive." Stephen's first biographer, F. W. Maitland, declared that the editor's decision to publish Henley's poems was one of his "boldest ventures."[16] But Stephen's acceptance was not without conditions. Quickly deleted from the proofs were portraits of a patient with a "rich, ripe whiskey-tinted nose," a nurse with "the sweetest violet eyes," and a scrubber with "a mutch, a beard, a long false face." Excised from "Night Picture" were the feline cries of the poem's genesis.

Night Picture

Implacable, the speck of gas compels
  My fascinated eyes, and makes them sore;
  Perverse, the bedclothes ramble, more and more;
Like rockery the mattress sinks and swells.

The men are slumbering, but my soul rebels
  Against one resolute, sonorous snore;
  An opiated, exasperating roar,
The murder of my sweet first doze it knells.

Waking I dream. My sleep fancy plumbs
  The sea of my mishap; a cinder drops;
    The shadow pulses as the loud flames fret;

  My neighbour groans and turns; the snorer stops,
Chokes, gasps him free again; the night-nurse comes,
    Noiseless and strange: "Are ye no' sleepin' yet?"

The sequence—"Hospital Outlines: Sketches and Portraits"—was published in the July 1875 *Cornhill Magazine.*

Buoyed by the publication of the sonnets and by his discharge from the infirmary, Henley proceeded immediately to work on a second series of hospital poems. In the waning months of his sojourn in Lister's wards, suffering constantly from boredom, he had begun to experiment with free-verse forms to express his thoughts and feelings, especially his despair, and to explore incidents in his experience in which his subject was himself. He had been reading Balzac and Heine. In Balzac, he encountered a line—later retained as the epigraph to *In Hospital*—that expressed his situation exactly: "On ne saurait dire á quel point un homme, seul dans son lit et malade, devient personnel." In Heine's *Lazarus* he discovered a model for an unprogressive narrative, random yet poignant confessions of the sufferer's mental states. Convalescing at Portobello, Henley wrote to Stevenson, on May 29, 1875: "I am at work on the *Lazarus*."[17]

In a small notebook—given over to lines in Henley's hand of miscellaneous poetry and prose written in pencil and dated during the summer of 1875—are several drafts of poems identified by the inscription "Lazarus." Two of these, both dated July 14, are revisions of "Night Picture" and anticipations of "Vigil."

dark
In the long ~~night~~
Laid on my back & unable
Even to turn on my side
is
Life ~~seems~~ a horrible nightmare

Shoulders & loins
cudgelled
Ache as tho' ~~beaten~~. The mattress
Turned into rockery stretches
Horrid with jags & the gas-jet
Screwed to a tremulous peep
Fills my both eyes, like a sun,
Banishing sleep,
Filling my senses with hate & despair

All the old ~~life~~ time
Surges malignant before me.
All the old faces
twilight.
Loved & rejected, people the ~~shadows~~
And the new days
Pass in procession before me
Like a strange pageant of shadows
~~Looking~~ Stonily staring
Into the doubt of the future—
While all about me my fellows
Snore me to madness.

Sleep comes at last
                                        misgivings
Sleep, full of dreams & ~~desires~~
                    voices & sounds
Broken with ~~brutal harsh voices~~
~~Telling the presence of morn~~,
Brutal & mean &

. . . .

In the long dark
Laid on my back & unable
Even to ~~turn~~ move
Life is a horrible nightmare.

Shoulders & loins
Ache as tho' cudgelled. The mattress
Turned into rockery stretches
Horrid with jags, & the gas-jet
Screwed to a tremulous peep
Banishing sleep & with hatred
Charging my spirit.
While all about me my fellows
Snore me to madness.

All the old time
Surges malignant before me,
All the old faces
Loved & rejected, people the twilight.
All the new days
Pass in procession before me,
Like a strange pageant of shadows
Stonily staring
Into the doubt of the future.

Sleep comes at last
Sleep full of dreams & misgivings
Broken with voices & sounds
Brutal & mean,
Telling the presence of morn.

In these 'Lazarus' texts, Henley had abandoned the sonnet conventions and substituted free syntactic units to express his physical and mental anguish. Here external circumstances—"the mattress turned into rockery" and "the gas-jet screwed to a tremulous peep"—are presented as the perceptions of the poet, who is now the principal object of attention. Henley understood that these expressive lyrics challenged the prevailing canons of Victorian taste. "There is a second lot of Hospital stuff to come," he told Harry Nichols, "but I doubt it will ever see light till the author is one with the dark." [18]

Aside from the 'Lazarus' text, no manuscript of the second hospital series has survived. Yet it is certain that Henley sent fair copies of the poems to friends and that he submitted the work, by his own admission, to "every editor of standing in London." As early as July 17, three days after he composed the untitled drafts of "Vigil," he wrote to Stevenson: "If you send the Lazarus to Colvin, ask him to return it presently, as I want Stephen to have it by the beginning of August." [19] Among Sidney Colvin's papers—according to E. V. Lucas—was "the complete MS. of the second series of Henley's hospital poems . . . with a large number of suggested variations." [20] As this second series was submitted and rejected again and again, Henley changed its title from "Lazarus" to "Hospital Moments" to "Hospital Outlines." Offering the work to *Blackwood's,* he explained: "I have revised & rewritten a great part of the poem. It has no other synthesis than that of time & place. I was twenty months or so in the Infirmary, & I wished in writing these verses to treat the matter as subjectively as I could. And this I have done. . . . There is no word set down in my copy that is not true." [21] Returning the manuscript, John Blackwood consoled: "I am very sorry to say that I do not think you have been successful in the form or wording into which you have thrown the Hospital Moments. . . . I hope I may turn out to be quite wrong and that others may feel more poetry in the irregular unrhymed verse you have selected for your sad powerful pictures." [22] The best criticism—and the clearest distinction ever drawn between the first and second series of the hospital poems—Henley received not from an editor but from T. E.

Brown, his mentor, who read the "Hospital Moments" in January 1876:

> In the first set there is the repose of graphic art . . . an exquisitely delicate but supreme and absolute observation . . . an almost childlike reproduction of the object. Now these are, as you say, more subjective . . . and the most subjective (Night-Watcher) is the finest. . . . But it affects me more because I know out of what wine-press it has come than from its perfection as a work of art. . . . At present we look for the objective well carved and well coloured; and I am not sure that we are wrong. Hereafter it may be otherwise: *absit omen*! but what would the world have said if among the papers of poor Chatterton it had found such a poem as the Night Watcher![23]

Brown was correct in his assessment of contemporary critical attitudes. And Henley, unable to place the "Hospital Moments," suspended his poetic ambitions and turned to journalism for his subsistence.

It was not until 1887, when H. B. Donkin was compiling a charity volume—*Voluntaries for an East London Hospital*—that Henley's free-verse hospital lyrics were published. Of the thirteen "Hospital Sketches" printed by Donkin, four, including "Vigil," were selected from among the original 'Lazarus' drafts.

Vigil

Lived on one's back
In the long hours of repose,
Life is a nightmare,
A grimy, a horrible nightmare.

Shoulders and loins
Ache, and the mattresses,
Horrid with boulders and hummocks,
Burn, and the gas,
An inevitable atom of light,
Haunts me, and stertorous sleepers
Snore me to madness.

All the old time
Surges before me malignant.
Old faces, old kisses, old songs,
Blossom derisive about me.
While the new days
Pass me in endless procession:
A pageant of shadows
Silently, staringly wending
On to the future.

Sleep comes at last—
Sleep, full of dreams and misgivings,
Broken with brutal and sordid
Voices and sounds that impose on me,
Ere I can wake to it,
The unnatural, intolerable day.

Although the four lyrics printed by Donkin are more tightly structured in the *Voluntaries* version than in their original states, there is little evidence that Henley had revised them significantly. "Will you tell me what you think of 'em?" he asked Hamilton Bruce. "They lack finish, but they should interest you. They were written ten or a dozen years ago, & rejected on every side."[24]

Although the *Voluntaries* publication gave Henley little pleasure, interest in the hospital poems was stirring. Stevenson, in New York, submitted them to Scribner's, and while Scribner's editor E. L. Burlingame was considering them, Alfred Nutt—the London publisher—chanced upon them in the *Voluntaries* anthology. "Please send off Mr. Henley's verses to him at once," Stevenson urged Burlingame,[25] for Nutt had approached Henley and had offered to publish his poems. On November 10, 1887, Henley wrote to Austin Dobson: "I believe the book is now certain to come off."[26]

The nature and occasion of the final process of selection, of the conflation of the *Cornhill* sonnets and the *Voluntaries* lyrics, have been admirably told by Henley himself:

> After spending the better part of my life in the pursuit of poetry, I found myself (about 1877) so utterly unmarketable that I had to own myself beaten in art, and to addict myself to journalism for the next ten years. Came the production by my old friend, Mr. H. B. Donkin, in his little collection of "Voluntaries" . . . of those unrhyming rhythms in which I had tried to quintessentialize, as (I believe) one scarce can do in rhyme, my memories of the Old Edinburgh Infirmary. They had long since been rejected by every editor of standing in London—I had well-nigh said in the world; but as soon as Mr. Nutt had read them, he entreated me to look for more. I did as I was told; old dusty sheaves were dragged to light, the work of selection and correction was begun; I burned much; I found that, after all, the lyrical instinct had slept—not died; I ventured (in brief) "A Book of Verses."[27]

This process of "selection and correction" was indeed a triumph of the "lyrical instinct." Although the most prominent result of the conflation is the arrangement of the poems in a dramatic cycle, from "Enter Patient" to "Discharged," the more significant effect throughout is a heightened subjectivity and immediacy. For the final text of "Vigil," Henley revised only superficially the *Voluntaries* version. But he interposed here an additional stanza, the original "Night-Picture," including the nurse's whisper, the fellow patient's snoring, and, of course, the cat cries of the poem's genesis. The upshot is a remarkable tension between objectivity and subjectivity, extroversion and introspection, perception and participation. The fusion of these two modes of expression—dramatic and lyric—suggests that the meaning of the vigil resides not only in the situation but also within the poet himself.

Vigil

Lived on one's back,
In the long hours of repose,
Life is a practical nightmare—
Hideous, asleep or awake.

Shoulders and loins
Ache—!
Ache, and the mattress,
Run into boulders and hummocks,
Glows like a kiln, while the bed-clothes—
Tumbling, importunate, daft—
Ramble and roll, and the gas,
Screwed to its lowermost,
An inevitable atom of light,
Haunts, and a stertorous sleeper
Snores me to hate and despair.

All the old time
Surges malignant before me;
Old voices, old kisses, old songs
Blossom derisive about me;
While the new days
Pass me in endless procession:
A pageant of shadows
Silently, leeringly wending
On . . . and still on . . . still on!
Far in the stillness a cat
Languishes loudly. A cinder
Falls, and the shadows
Lurch to the leap of the flame. The next man to me
Turns with a moan; and the snorer,
The drug like a rope at his throat,
Gasps, gurgles, snorts himself free, as the night-nurse,
Noiseless and strange, Her bull's-eye half-lanterned in apron,
(Whispering me, "Are ye no sleepin' yet?")
Passes, list-slippered and peering,
Round . . . and is gone.

Sleep comes at last—
Sleep full of dreams and misgivings—
Broken with brutal and sordid
Voices and sounds
That impose on me, ere I can wake to it,
The unnatural, intolerable day.

This history of one poem—which began as "Night Thoughts," proceeded apace to "Night Sketch," "Night Picture," and "Night Watcher," and concluded as "Vigil"—illustrates the ironic pattern of the composition and revision of *In Hospital.* In the infirmary, in immediate response to actual events, Henley directed his attention to external circumstances and established their authenticity by objectifying his perceptions. As the years passed, however, and as Henley's comprehension of his hospital experience became increasingly retrospective, his revisory tendency was to express his perceptions with increasing spontaneity and subjectivity. In its completed form, the sequence is both presented and understood as Henley's expression and perception, as his experience, as a life within his life.

NOTES

1. 32:120–28.
2. (London: David Stott), pp. 130–48.
3. (London: David Nutt), pp. 1–48.
4. Henley Archive (MA 1617), Pierpont Morgan Library. Hereafter cited as "Pierpont Morgan Library."
5. The Stevenson Library of Edwin J. Beinecke, Beinecke Rare Book and Manuscript Library, Yale University. Hereafter cited as "Beinecke Library."
6. The most comprehensive accounts of Henley's hospital life appear in Jerome H. Buckley's *William Ernest Henley: A Study in the "Counter-Decadence" of the 'Nineties* (Princeton, N.J.: Princeton University Press, 1945), pp. 42–55; John Connell's *W. E. Henley* (London: Constable, 1949), pp. 49–88; and Andre Guillaume's *William Ernest Henley et son groupe* (Paris: Klincksieck, 1973), pp. 29–59.
7. "Mr. Henley's Poetry," *Fortnightly Review,* n.s., 52 (1892): 185.
8. See Edward H. Cohen, "Uncollected Early Poems by William Ernest Henley," *Bulletin of the New York Public Library* 79 (1976): 297–314.
9. Dated April 18, 1873, Letters of William Ernest Henley to Harry Nichols, Huntington Library, HM 30919. Hereafter cited as "Huntington Library."
10. Huntington Library, HM 30922.
11. Dated February 12, 1875. Quoted by Frederic William Maitland, *The Life and Letters of Leslie Stephen* (London: Duckworth, 1906), p. 250.
12. Dated February 12, 1875, National Library of Scotland, MS 99, folio 60.
13. Undated, Beinecke Library, MS 8401.
14. Beinecke Library, MS 4693.
15. Beinecke Library, MS 4695.
16. Maitland, p. 266.
17. Beinecke Library, MS 4699.

18. Huntington Library, HM 30929.

19. Beinecke Library, MS 4700.

20. E. V. Lucas, *The Colvins and Their Friends* (London: Methuen, 1928), p. 115.

21. Dated February 9, 1877, National Library of Scotland, Blackwood Papers, MS 4360, folio 207.

22. Dated February 21, 1877, William Blackwood and Sons, Private Letter Book (May 1874–March 1877), folio 546.

23. Pierpont Morgan Library.

24. Uncatalogued letter dated June 22, 1887, Beinecke Library.

25. Beinecke Library, MS 2904.

26. Quoted by Connell, p. 107.

27. William Ernest Henley, *Poems by William Ernest Henley* (London: Nutt, 1898), pp. vii–viii.

7

Browning and How He Worked in Good Temper*

Ashby Bland Crowder

In 1876 Robert Browning published *Pacchiarotto and How He Worked in Distemper: with Other Poems.* In the title poem of this volume Browning answers the critics who had been nipping at him for decades, and at the end of it Browning threatens that his housemaid (his muse) might toss the slops from a *skoramis* (chamber pot) upon their heads. The image of a chamber pot so used is generally thought to be humorous, as it is in Candide's encounter with a Dutch religious zealot or in a similar scene in *Joseph Andrews* by Henry Fielding.

It is no surprise, however, that Browning's critics were not amused. They did not like his attitude. And they took what he had to say to them very seriously—and responded very seriously. According to the *Saturday Review* Browning's criticism of the critics was "unprovoked," "unreasonable," "coarse," and an indication of "puerile vanity."[1] The *Graphic* implied that Browning's publication of *Pacchiarotto* revealed "a perverted in-

*Reprinted from *Browning Institute Studies* 17 (1989): 93–113.

genuity" as well as "ill-temper, spiritual pride, and even, possibly, bad taste."[2] Those friendly to Browning have tried to gloss over what he said in the poem. Edward Berdow, for example, issues an ultra-Victorian euphemism to hide the reality of Browning's offense: his *Browning Cyclopaedia* identifies the *skoramis* as "a vessel of dishonour."[3] But most of his contemporary reviewers thought Browning a very angry man who had no business venting his anger in a public poem.

Since Browning's time, critics have concluded that perhaps the poet ought to have thought twice about the *Pacchiarotto* volume. William Lyon Phelps pronounced the title poem "an error in judgment."[4] Norton Crowell has called it "one of the most mordant satires of the nineteenth century," judging the personal criticism of the critic Alfred Austin as "perhaps unworthy of the great poet."[5] More recently William Irvine and Park Honan have seen "Pacchiarotto" as evidence of "a growing perversity not wholly attributable to old age, a new failure in self-control and more deeply in self-assurance."[6]

I am inclined, however, to agree with Clyde Ryals, who sees the poem "Pacchiarotto" as "a lively and amusing affair full of rollicking good humor."[7] Indeed, speaking in his own person in the poem, Browning makes clear his own tone. He whistles while he works (l. 496)[8]; he begins his story "with a chuckle" and in the end announces that he has "laughed out my laugh on this mirth-day!" (ll. 538, 572). As for the charge that in "Pacchiarotto" Browning exhibits a lapse of self-control, I find instead that Browning's manuscript[9] and the subsequent revisions point to a composed mind that had control over its emotions in answering the charges of the critics. Although the poet worked rapidly, finishing the 581-line poem in just two weeks' time,[10] he afterward gave a great deal of thoughtful attention to the improvement of his original draft, and this thoughtful attention continued as he revised for the 1876 edition. During these two stages, he thoroughly reworked key passages and added lines in order to clarify meaning and action, introduce visual and auditory power, and in various ways sharpen his measured denunciation of his critics. He also carried out small-scale revisions that yielded smoother lines, metrical appropriateness, and simple clarity and strength of expression. Punctuation was his concern especially as he revised for the 1876 edition. Though he gave only slight attention to the poem when preparing for *The Poetical Works of Robert Browning,* published in 1888–89,[11] these few revisions too are thoughtful and do improve the text. Indeed, it is Pacchiarotto, the poem's ill-humored reformer meant to parallel literary critic Alfred Austin, who worked in distemper. Browning himself worked in very good temper. In the remainder of the essay I examine the effects of his revisions in, first, the manuscript, then the proofs of the first edition (1876), and the final edition (1888–89).

MANUSCRIPT REVISIONS

There are three significant passages to which Browning gave his extraordinary attention when he revised initially. The most heavily revised part of the manuscript contains Pacchiarotto's speech to the Bardotti, the party of radical reformers in Siena (of which this painter is a member) who had assembled to debate what should be done to help Siena through a famine. All told, there are thirty-six word substitutions or alterations carried out on the manuscript page containing Pacchiarotto's political speech. Some of these word changes I shall take up later on; first I should like to focus on the eleven lines added to the speech in Section 15 of the poem.[12] Browning first tried adding three of the lines at the beginning of Pacchiarotto's address, changed his mind, then added seven lines to those three, and inserted all ten lines later in the speech. Then he added another line above the long insert. Browning's intentions in these additions are, I think, clear. The additional lines clarify the dramatic context and establish motivation for action—motivation that had originally been uncertain.

The line additions first occur as Pacchiarotto criticizes the city government for inadequacy in dealing with the crisis:

> He harangued on the faults of the Bailiwick,

the narrator says. Browning tentatively decided to replace this line with a three-line address that Pacchiarotto offers directly to the city's governors:

> Oh, Magistrates out on ye all! Fie,
> Thou Chief of our forces, Amalfi
> Who shieldest the rogue & clotpoll.[13]

Then Browning decided not to make Pacchiarotto address the magistrates directly—a wise decision, since in fact Pacchiarotto stands not before the magistrates but before the Bardotti, who had assembled in order to castigate the government and to argue among themselves about solutions to the problems of the city. Therefore Browning deliberately returned the original l. 251, "He harangued on the faults of the Bailiwick," making it clear that what follows is an address to the Bardotti. Instead, then, of the direct address "Oh, Magistrates . . .," Browning made Pacchiarotto say to the reformers, "If you shout, Bailiff . . ." (l. 264), and then Pacchiarotto proceeds to tell them what they ought to shout to the bailiff.

In the lines that follow the restored l. 251, Pacchiarotto complains especially about the inadequate education of the ruling classes whose knowledge is the useless "pedantry picked up at college / From Doctors, Professors *et cetera*" (ll. 256–57). He suggests that classical studies amount to nothing more than a "string of *kappas, taus,* [and] *lambdas,* / [being] Tacked on to the tail of each damned ass." Immediately then Browning, in the original manuscript version, allowed Pacchiarotto to jump ahead with his proposal of what is needed:

> But knowledge indeed—practicality!
> Through insight's fine universality—
> If you listened to me. . . .

For offering a practical approach to the problems of Siena and for starting to suggest that he himself possessed some of the needed practical wisdom, Pacchiarotto is attacked by the Bardotti, and he is forced to run for his life. Recognizing that Pacchiarotto's intentions seemed very little provocation for such a violent reaction, Browning added seven lines to the three beginning with "If you shout, Bailiff," which had been inserted at the start of the speech, and then moved all ten lines to the end of the address. He did this in order to give a clearer meaning to

"If you listened to me . . ." (l. 274). The newly grouped addition, in which Pacchiarotto tries to stir up the radicals to overthrow the government, reads as follows:

> If you shout, Bailiffs, out on ye all! Fie,
> Thou Chief of our forces, Amalfi
> Who shieldest the rogue & clotpoll.
> If you pounce on and poke out, with what pole
> I leave ye to fancy, our Siena's
> Beast-litter of Sloths and hyenas
> (Who ever to scan this is ill able
> Forgets the town's name's a dissyllable)
> If, this done, ye did—as ye might—place
> For once the right man in the right place.
> (ll. 264–73)

And now the new meaning for "If you listened to me . . ." comes into existence. It is clear that the Bardotti understand Pacchiarotto's proposal that they establish *him* as the practical-minded chief magistrate who will lead the city out of all its difficulties. The sheer arrogance of this reformer seems now provocation enough for the members of his own group to pounce on him.

Apparently Browning then added another line that amplifies Pacchiarotto's denunciation of the Sienese magistrates, thereby establishing more firmly the painter's view of himself as the only proper alternative. After Pacchiarotto speaks of the bits of classical knowledge "Tacked on to the tail of each damned ass," Browning inserted interlinearly:

> No knowledge we want of this quality—

before Pacchiarotto refers to the practical knowledge he himself would supply were *he* the leader. This line, then, furnishes an effective preparation to the series of ten lines already discussed.

The story of the self-important reformer Pacchiarotto is meant to suggest a parallel between the Sienese painter and the critic and poet Alfred Austin, who wished very much to reform Browning. Browning then turned to attack his critics—especially Austin—directly. For years, led by Austin, critics had harped on Browning's alleged discordant obscurities. Austin had been especially abusive and unfair; according to Browning, Austin was guilty in his reviews of "misquoting passages and designedly leaving out words or lines so as to make absolute nonsense of them."[14] Therefore Browning was ready to display to Austin the "biting wit" that Austin had accused the poet of having.[15]

This personal mode was uncustomary to Browning, and he at first faltered before resuming control. In fact, in Sections 24–26 Browning changed or altered forty-four words, gave some attention to punctuation revision, and inserted seven lines as he created an additional section of the poem. These revisions contribute an essential visual and auditory power as well as clarity to the passage.

Speaking in his own person, Browning imagines greeting the ragtag bunch of his critics that has accosted him early in the morning. He describes the motley crew as being dressed in "reds,[16] blues and yellows"—colors which are also the colors of the periodicals that reviewed Browning's poetry. But in order to add detail on the realistic level, he inserted a line that visually characterizes his critics as burlesque entertainers with "saltbox and bones, tongs and bellows" (l. 465).

Next, where the leader of the band of critics steps forward and announces, "We critics as sweeps out your chimbly!" (l. 469), Browning playfully added four lines in the right margin that develop the allegorical function of the critic-sweeps. The critic-sweeps say,

> Much soot to remove from your flue, Sir,
> Who spares coal in kitchen an't you, Sir,
> And neighbours complain it's no joke, Sir,
> —You ought to consume your own smoke, Sir!
> (ll. 470–73)

This criticism furnishes Browning with an opportunity to make a forceful answer. His most telling defense of his own poetry is against the common charge that he has a "tough-gristled" (l. 494) ear and thus cannot produce a musical or rhythmically satisfying line. Browning's defense is based on a comparison between himself and two famous composers. In the first instance, referring to the deaf Beethoven, Browning originally wrote[17]:

> Whereby, tap, tap, tap, tap, 'tis proven
> I know it [music] no more than Beethoven.

The first line of this couplet is so monotonous as to undermine the intended irony of the second. Recognizing that the four "taps" would not do, Browning altered the line as follows, vastly improving its sound-effects:

> Whereby, tap-tap, chink-chink, 'tis proven
> (l. 490)

In the second line the poet muted the irony and substituted a forceful positive statement that makes the poet and the musician fellow rule-breakers and sets them well above the measuring critics who base their judgments solely upon formula:

> I break rule as bad as Beethoven.

Browning next inserted in the right margin a couplet that establishes a parallel between the poet and his innovative and much-misunderstood contemporary Schumann. In fact, a real-life critic had already noted a parallel between Browning and Schumann. Reviewing *Aristophanes' Apology*, the *Pall Mall Gazette* had written: "perhaps a parallel between Schumann's music and Mr. Browning's poetry might be found not too fanciful if anyone chose to pursue it." [18] Surely remembering this review from several months earlier, Browning imagined the critics asking,

> "That chord now—a groan or a grunt is't?
> Schumann's self was no worse contrapuntist?"
> (ll. 492–93)[19]

It seems obvious that Browning means for this insertion to bolster his defense of his own prosodic methods.

The next section that required an extraordinary amount of revision begins just past the middle of Section 27, and the trouble turns on issues of special consequence at the very end of the section, which is also heavily revised. First of all, near the midway point of this section Browning added three rhymed lines in order to help clarify the contrast that he meant to establish between the critics and the poet. At this point in the poem, Browning has already compared the critics to chimney sweeps who make their kind of music by banging drums and rattling their brushes; these are the very critics who accuse Browning of having no ear for music. Browning shouts to the assemblage of ragtag critics, who are still gathered below his window:

> . . . here shall my whistling and singing
> Set all the street's echoes a-ringing
> Long after the last of your number
> Has ceased my front-court to encumber.
> (ll. 514–17)

The contrast between the enduring nature of the poet's utterance and fleeting song of the critics is emphasized in the triplet that Browning then added:

> While, treading down rose and ranunculus
> You *Tommy-make-room-for-your-uncle*-us
> So, all of you—man or homunculus.
> (ll. 518–20)

Then, as a character in the poem, Browning orders them to march away. First, Browning has turned the title of the popular song "Tommy Make Room for Your Uncle" into a verb that emphasizes the meanness and outrageousness of what the critics have done: they have produced a low-quality song themselves, and they in general possess powers of discrimination so meager as to make it impossible for them to tell the difference between good music or poetry (a rose) and undistinguished music or poetry (a ranunculus, which is a wild flower). Therefore, they trample rose and ranunculus alike, says Browning. In strengthening his denunciation of his critics, Browning took the opportunity to allude humorously to Austin's small stature, calling him "a homunculus."[20] Having urged the critics to be gone, Browning warns that his housemaid, named Xanthippe after the bad-tempered wife of Socrates, might dump on their heads a souse of foul composition. Browning changed rather remarkably his manner of expressing this threat. He first wrote,

> Quick march, for Xantippe [*sic*], my housemaid
> If once on your pates she a souse made
> With what in the way of utensil
> First comes to her hand . . Pacchia's pencil.

In revision Browning strengthened the threat, making it clearer exactly what Xantippe will throw upon the critics:

> Quick march, for Xantippe, my housemaid
> If once on your pates she a souse made
> With what, pan or pot, bowl or skoramis
> First comes to her hand . . things were more amiss!
> (ll. 521–24)

Having established the expectation that Austin will be wiping the contents of a chamber pot from his face, and having carried off the hilarious rhyme of "skoramis" and "more amiss," Browning was pretty much satisfied with this passage—except for its conclusion.[21]

Browning's difficulty with the very end of this section is indicated not by the revisions he made but by those he failed to make. In fact, he had so much trouble with the conclusion to Section 27 that he left the last two lines unresolved. He could not settle on how to conclude the section effectively until he revised the proofs for the first edition. In the line just before the last two of the section, Browning, after several false starts, produced the following line that begins to conclude his attack on his enemy, Austin:

> I've discharged on his pate his own verses—
> (l. 532)[22]

On the manuscript Browning originally followed up this line with the following conclusion to the section:

As if they should touch my utensil!

Before he wrote the next line, he changed it to read,

As if they should touch an utensil

followed by

Of mine—do thy slops such immense ill!

Dissatisfied with this conclusion, Browning crossed out words but never got the lines back to the point where they made good sense. The final manuscript reading for this couplet remains fragmentary:

As if they an utensil
Of mine—do thy slops such immense ill!

Apparently, while marking the proofs, however, Browning arrived at an alternative couplet that must have satisfied him in the extreme: it allowed him another opportunity to make fun of Austin's small stature and to associate himself with another eminent writer who had winced under the small man's unfair attack:

"Dwarfs are saucy," says Dickens: so, sauced in
Your own sauce, . . .* [asterisk and ellipsis marks are in Browning's text]

(ll. 533–34)

And the reader knows that the name "Alfred Austin" is required to complete the rhyme. But apparently even this aspersion was not enough to satisfy Browning, for he made the unprecedented decision to add an ironic footnote that purports to amplify the joke about Austin's smallness. The gleeful footnote interrupts as follows:

*No, please! For
"Who would be satirical
On a thing so very small?"—PRINTER'S DEVIL.[23]

It is overwhelmingly clear that Browning means for us to understand that *he* would!

Knowing that he needed to change the manuscript lines

ending in "utensil" and "immense ill" when he read the proofs, Browning anticipated the necessity of rescuing the first line of the next section, a line that had originally made a transitional triplet, ending in "Pencil," but which was destined to stand with no corresponding rhyme in a poem composed entirely of couplets and triplets. Therefore, Browning added a line to make the following couplet:

> But back to my Knight of the Pencil,
> Dismissed to his fresco and stencil—[24]
> (ll. 535–36)

The added line both completes the rhyme and makes the return to Pacchiarotto more concrete as it places him once again in his home with the figures he painted on the wall.

Beyond these three areas of concentrated revision on the manuscript, Browning made several other sorts of changes. All told, thirty-eight lines were added to the manuscript, either interlinearly or marginally. Browning seems to have added most of these lines to provide effective detail; others appear to be required to complete an idea.

The addition of effective details for clarification seems the commonest reason that the poet inserted lines. For example, after Pacchiarotto has railed against the painted figures on the wall of his grotto in an imaginative effort to reform them, he is disposed to provide excuses for his figures' behavior or shortcomings. At first, Pacchiarotto excused his priest's insipid sermons (the priest "tells us stuff he was reared in . . .") and then went immediately on to the excuses for his soldier's inadequacies. The revised manuscript begins Pacchiarotto's defense of the priest with two additonal lines, which make his fallibility clearer:

> The Priest—who expects him to descant
> On duty with more zeal and less cant?
> (ll. 140–41)

A little further on in the episode Pacchiarotto mentions some of the vanities of women and then defends them with this question:

What's their frailty beside our falsehood?
(l. 157)

To this vague and general line, Browning added three lines that turn this one ironic; they add telling detail and ambiguity, providing offense within the context of defense:

The baldest, most brazen of . . . trumpets,
How kind can they be to their dumb pets!
Of their charms—how are all frank, how few venal!
(ll. 158–60)[25]

The reader is of course meant to supply an initial "s" to make "trumpets" into "strumpets," though he might also refrain from doing so and hear only a woman sounding her own praises. Then the kindness to "dumb pets" that Pacchiarotto praises in particular leaves women's general unkindness undefended. Though the final of the three lines purports to be a defense, the very idea that a charm can be venal is startling, even if only a few of them are.

The addition of lines simply to clarify the point of a passage occurs in the speech the Abbot makes to Pacchiarotto. The Abbot admonishes the painter to give up vain hopes of reforming the world; heaven is where the shortcomings of this life will be overcome. He argues that we should therefore work without hope of succeeding, "Because if success were intended / Why, heaven would begin ere earth ended"; and then, according to the original manuscript version, he says, "Earth's a mill where we grind and wear mufflers" (ll. 373–4, 377). The force of the priest's final metaphor is clarified and strengthened by Browning's insertion (in the right margin) of the following couplet:

A Free-Horse? Be rather a thill-horse,
Or—what's the plain truth—just a mill-horse!
(ll. 375–76)

This expansion of the horse metaphor gives clarity and force to the Abbot's urgent advice to Pacchiarotto that he should abandon the Bardotti (a later revision calls them Spare-Horses) and become a shaft-horse, one that works, or even a mill-horse, one that works even though it does so without any freedom.

The improvements that Browning achieved through the addition of lines to the manuscript are clear. Yet one can best see the enormous care that the poet took when revising his manuscript in the small changes to individual lines: these produced smoother lines and increased clarity, precision, and concrete detail. Browning's focus can perhaps best be observed in what might be considered his most minor alterations—those carried out to achieve a smoother poetic line. He improved the poetic quality of the poem, for example, by uncrimping awkward lines: "provoking / The nicer throats to coughing nay choking" becomes "The nicer throat's coughing and choking" (l. 221). And although often roundly attacked by his critics for metrical carelessness, Browning actually took great care in revising for metrical effectiveness. During the section in which Pacchiarotto makes up excuses for the "behavior" of his painted characters, as a result of two lines added to the manuscript, it became unnecessary in the line following to repeat the words "The Priest." Substituting "He" for these two words, however, threw the meter off; therefore Browning substituted "but rubbish" for "stuff" in order to pick up lost syllables in the following line, keeping it from being jarringly short: "He preaches but rubbish he's reared in" (l. 142).

Although the critics unremittingly accused Browning of willful obscurity, he used great care making his poem clearer. Some of these revisions for clarity are directed at overcoming the most obvious sorts of uncertainties of expression. For example, when Browning first wrote that the *aubades* did their "best to amuse—nor was so bad!" he saw that he had omitted mentioning who was meant to be amused by the *aubades,* and so he added the word "me" after "to amuse."[26] In another such instance Browning reformed an ill-wrought, inexact statement into a clear one. At first he had written that "each personage [was] painted / On the chamber with which you're acquainted" but recast the statement as follows:

> . . . each personage [is] painted
> On wall sides where with you're acquainted.
> (ll. 249–50)[27]

Browning's interest in clarity meant that he was willing to curb his strong inclination for metaphor when it got in the way of his meaning. Having first written, " . . . behold, Pacchiarotto, / The end thy beginning has got to," he elected to introduce a metaphor, revising as follows: " . . . behold, Pacchiarotto, / The pass which thy road has got to." But he trimmed half this metaphor away in order to make a clearer expression: " . . . behold, Pacchiarotto, / The pass which thy project has got to" (ll. 291–92).

Word substitutions done to achieve vivid detail and immediacy are among the most striking that Browning carried out. Some of these revisions are simply a matter of his introducing a specific word, one that immediately stimulates the visual imagination, as when he has his eloquent Abbot ask, " . . . there may linger / A pimple I fray with rough finger [?] " (ll. 392–93). That pimple we see; it is less likely that we could see the more generalized "scar" that Browning originally had the Abbot say. At other times Browning achieved immediacy by striking weak verbs and substituting strong ones indicating action. The examples are many. Browning at first said that Pacchiarotto's "voice . . . had shamed Boanerges. . . ," but revision gave Pacchiarotto a "voice that out-roared Boanerges . . ." (l. 132). Elsewhere the narrator stated that a "mouth, for a combat itchy, / Had no trouble with that convincing / Reply. . . ." Eliminating the feeble "Had no trouble," Browning introduced a verb that gave life to the lines:

> . . . mouth, for the combat itchy,
> Quivers with the convincing
> Reply. . . .
>
> (ll. 111–13)

Next, Browning eliminated the ordinary verb "spoke" in referring to the group of radical political reformers that Pacchiarotto belonged to and provided instead a verb that plays on the fact that Bardotti means "free-horses" or "spare-horses." The radicals' views were first introduced as follows:

> This Company forthwith assembled:
> Spoke words whereat citizens trembled.

Successful revision produced:

> These Free Horses forthwith assembled:
> Neighed words whereat citizens trembled.
> (ll. 233–34)[28]

The most obvious strengthening of the poetry by the change of a single word is, not surprisingly, associated with revisions involving the verb *to be.* Pacchiarotto originally said to the Abbot: "Yet be not discouraged, O Father." Wisely, Browning revised the verb as follows: "Yet blush not discouraged, O Father" (l. 404).[29] In another instance Browning contradicted expectations and achieved a more forceful expression by introducing the ordinarily weak verb *to be.* (He also substituted the more abstract "proved" for the more concrete "worked.") He had first written,

> And if men prefer to live foolishly,
> At least we worked horse-like not mulishly. . . .

which he revised as follows:

> And if men prefer to be foolish,
> Ourselves have proved horse-like not mulish.
> (ll. 385–86)

The poet must have felt compelled to make these revisions because they would allow him to change two adverbs into adjectives and thereby arrive at a tighter, more forceful two lines.

THE FIRST EDITION (1876)

In spite of all the revisions carried out on the manuscript of "Pacchiarotto," Browning nonetheless had some matters of considerable significance to attend to after the poem had been set in type for the first edition (1876). He continued revisions and additions for the sake of clarity, forceful and vivid expression, and the elimination of awkwardness; he completed an incomplete line; and having paid little mind to punctuation on the manuscript, he gave serious attention, as was his usual practice, to commas, dashes, and exclamation marks while correcting the proofs.

Of all revisions done for the 1876 edition, which in general were evenly distributed throughout the poem, the most important are the line additions and substitutions. The first edition contains nine new lines: three lines substituted in the text, three added to the text, and three added in the form of a footnote. These are concentrated in the last three pages of the first edition. It will be recalled that the poet left the final couplet of Section 27 in a state of unfinished revision and that he abandoned his initial efforts to produce a pair of lines that ridiculed Alfred Austin. As we have already seen, he produced the couplet "Dwarfs are saucy," says Dickens: so sauced in / Your own sauce, . . ." as well as a three-line footnote while reading the proofs.

Twenty-three lines into the next section (28) Browning found another line that had to be scrapped. Speaking of his critics as horses limited to the "paddock / Of language allotted [them] *ad hoc*," he asked them:

> Pace still to and fro, forsooth, scorners
> Of those free of all its four corners?[30]

Striking the first of these two lines, Browning eliminated a halting and inelegant line and produced a forceful one that vividly emphasizes the limitations of his critics at whom the line points with the second-person pronoun:

> With a clog at your fetlocks,—you—scorners
> Of me free of all its four corners?[31]
> (ll. 558–59)

Then there are three lines that Browning added to the end of the poem. On the manuscript he had completed his attack on his critics with an announcement that he is not quite irritated by them:

> . . . I'm vexed here
> By no sweep, that's certain, till next year!
> (ll. 577–78)

In adding three lines to the 1876 edition, Browning goes a step further in the delineation of his mood: not only is he not at present vexed, but he is thankful, it seems, that his critics have roused him to write during a period that might otherwise have been a time of unproductive relaxation. Not being of a mind to sleep after accomplishing an important talk, like Pheidippides did, Browning links himself with his favorite Greek dramatist, Euripides, who was treated with hostility by his critics, implying that the criticism keeps Browning (as it kept Euripides) up and working. To this effect, he added the following:

> "Vexed?" roused from what else were insipid ease!
> Leave snoring a-bed to Pheidippides!
> We'll up and work! won't we, Euripides?
> (ll. 579–81)

These line additions and substitutions in particular represent the good temper with which Browning worked. He also engaged in a fair amount of word substitution and deletion while marking the first-edition proof sheets. The intentions behind those changes seem generally commensurate with those carried out on the manuscript, especially when Browning avoided awkwardness and when he sought clarity and vividness.

One of the examples of awkwardness overcome involves a line that Browning had trouble with at the manuscript stage. He originally tried to use the word "mankind" but found it too awkward to handle in his line of poetry:

> And as for mankind—let them all stick.

Aware, I suppose, of the critics poised to pounce on any grammatical indiscretion, he tried the generic "men," which would have worked pretty well—only he changed his pronoun, producing another awkwardness:

> And as for men—let each and all stick.
> (l. 448)

The "each" referring to "men," in spite of the "all" that followed, was unacceptable. Therefore, for the first edition he changed "men" to "Man," capitalizing it to make the generic intent clearer.

Browning also substituted words to clarify or enlarge his

meaning and to gain greater precision. At the beginning of the second part of "Pacchiarotto," when Browning addresses the band of critics that has aroused him from his sleep, he first described the critics as being dressed in "reds, blues and yellows." As the *Saturday Review* was to note, these colors represent the *Quarterly, Edinburgh,* and other literary journals containing criticism of Browning.[32] For the first edition Browning substituted "drabs" for "reds." "Drabs" expands the number of magazines he might mean, for *drab* refers to several shades of light brown, from light olive to grayish yellowish brown. Further, *drab* in the plural was Victorian usage for clothing of a drab color,[33] and thus it strengthens the image of the incongruously dressed assemblage below the poet's window and makes them less attractively and brightly dressed. In another instance Browning clarified the meaning by substituting "but" for "till." Early on in the Abbot's speech to Pacchiarotto, Browning originally had him say:

> I talked and wrote till, one morning,
> The Autumn bore fruit in this warning. . . .

which suggests that the talking and writing led eventually to a realization. The revision, however, makes it clear that the realization occurs independently of the talking and writing:

> I talked and I wrote, but, one morning,
> Life's Autumn bore fruit in this warning.
> (ll. 364–65)

Other word changes show Browning of a mind to draw sharper attention to his critics, and so in marking the proofs he inserted the word *critics* in addressing them directly. At first he had said simply, "Come back and . . . not shake hands, excuse me!" For the first edition he changed that line to "Come, critics,—not shake hands, excuse me!" (l. 542). The poet also inserted the word *critics* into the mouths of the critics themselves: instead of " 'Tis we, sir, as sweeps your chimbly" (manuscript), we have "We critics as sweeps your chimbly!" (l. 469). More remarkable is a revision that points more specifically to Alfred Austin's smallness. On the manuscript, Browning refers to "my

Hop-o'-my-thumb there, / Banjo-Byron. . . ." On the proof sheet he added an allusion to the dwarf in Dickens's *Old Curiosity Shop:* "as for Quilp-Hop-o'-my-thumb there" (l. 529).

In revising for the first edition, Browning continued his effort to eliminate less-than-precise verbs by substituting appropriate active verbs. This practice can best be observed in his revisions that emphasize the frantic manner of the Sienese painter. As Pacchiarotto goes off to the meeting of the Bardotti, Browning originally wrote: "Off to these at full speed set our worthy." Wanting to draw attention to Pacchiarotto's haste, however, Browning struck "set," replacing it with "rushed" (l. 244). On the other hand, two lines further on, to describe Pacchiarotto's approach to the rostrum from which he was to make his disastrous speech, Browning crossed out "rushed" and restored the first manuscript reading, "mounted," as we have seen. A few lines later, as he described Pacchiarotto's tactics of escape, Browning found "dash" an apt substitution for "rush"; it preserves the sense of confusion and haste but more precisely describes the nature of his movement: "Right and left did he dash helter-skelter" (l. 296). Further on, "clutch" takes the place of "take" (l. 399).

In other instances Browning inserted appropriate verbs that emphasize the action already present in the context. Addressing the motley band of critics, Browning, according to the manuscript, said,

> So, all of you—man or homunculus,
> Quick march! . . .

The proof revision replaces "So" with an action word appropriate to the context: "Troop, all of you . . ." (l. 520). Some lines later Browning inserted a verb form that parodies the action of the critics he describes; he eliminated "Who—even in that bit of the paddock" in favor of "You,—pacing in even that paddock" (l. 555). And he forewent "setting," replacing it with "cocking" in the following allusion to Pacchiarotto's manner of wearing his headgear: "Then, cocking (in Scotch phrase) his cap a-gee" (l. 165). Finally, instead of the original "at week's end, is my birthday," he substituted a verb of action: "Beside, at week's end, dawns my birthday" (l. 572).

Having paid little attention to regularizing punctuation while revising the manuscript, Browning engaged in this housekeeping duty while examining the first edition proof pages. He did not find it necessary to correct numerous mistakes, as he had done while going over the proofs of *The Inn Album,* where for example, he had made numerous misuses of the apostrophe.[34] Occasionally with "Pacchiarotto" he had to insert the comma required in direct address, phrases of contrast, a series, and before a coordinating conjunction followed by an independent clause. Most of his attention to punctuation, however, was given to deleting the dashes freely used during rapid composition and replacing them with more appropriate marks of punctuation—full stops, semicolons, and colons. By 1876 Browning had overcome, it seems, his penchant for the exclamation mark, which he had made a special effort to curb while revising for the first edition of *The Inn Album* (1875).[35] In fact, he found it necessary to add a few to "Pacchiarotto"—in obviously exclamatory statements like "I've discharged on his pate his own verses!" (l. 532). Finally, he transformed some declarative statements into interrogatives by adding the question mark, at the same time adding question marks to some sentences in which their absence was an obvious oversight.

THE FINAL EDITION (1888–89)

It has become clear that at the time he wrote "Pacchiarotto" and again as he read the proof sheets for the first edition, Browning took a strong interest in revising his poem. When he oversaw the publication of *The Poetical Works of Robert Browning* (1888–89), however, he did very little in the way of revising "Pacchiarotto." Either he was overwhelmingly satisfied with his original effort or he had lost interest in what he might have considered just a bit of passing fun. I tend to land on the first explanation as more likely, because as few as the revisions for the 1889 edition are, they reveal that the poet's critical intelligence was attentively directed at the poem.

That the poet would take the trouble to restore to the final edition an exclamation mark, contained in the manuscript but lost in the first edition, suggests more than a casual attitude toward the poem. He reintroduces the mark to line 461: "Droll dogs, as I jumped up, cried 'Heyday![']" Furthermore, he went through the poem and changed every incidence of *folks* to *folk* so that his usage would be consistent throughout the poem and, at the same time, conform to standard nineteenth-century form (*folks* was usual before the Victorian period). Beyond these, there were only four alterations made for the revised edition.

The transposition of lines 49 and 50 is the only final-edition revision mentioned by DeVane.[36] It is a very thoughtful alteration of the text, one that groups a pair of lines in a clearer and more logical manner. In the first edition, the narrator, describing the painter's penchant for reforming the whole improperly created world, says:

> And it struck him as expedient—
> Ere he tried to make obedient,
> By piping advice in one key
> The wolf, fox, bear and monkey—
> That his pipe should play a prelude.

The more logical and clearer revised edition reads as follows:

> Ere he tried to make obedient
> The wolf, fox, bear and monkey,
> By piping advice in one key—
> That his pipe should play a prelude.
> (ll. 48–51)

Elsewhere Browning inserted the verb "taught" to strengthen the narrator's introduction of Pacchiarotto's address to the figures painted on his wall. The 1876 version,

> He addressed in a choice oration
> His folk of each name and nation
> On the duties of every station. . . .

was improved as follows:

He addressed in a choice oration
His folk of each name and nation,
Taught its duties to every station.
(ll. 91–93)

Then, as the narrator introduces the section containing the Abbot's speech to Pacchiarotto, Browning effected another significant improvement over the first edition's version. According to the 1876 edition, Section 21 opens with: "'Ah, Youth!' so might run the admonishment," and the wise advice follows. Apparently Browning saw two things wrong with this opening line: first, it had been ten lines since the narrator had indicated who would be offering the admonition, and that information needed to be restated; second, the "so might run" makes the whole speech hypothetical instead of real in the poem. In the simplest way, the poet revised the line to correct both of these deficiencies, producing a smoother line as well: "'Ah, Youth!' ran the Abbot's admonishment" (l. 358).

Finally, in the penultimate section Browning had referred to the "quack-quack" of the goose-critic. It seems odd that a man who kept geese would even temporarily put into their beaks the sound of the duck. Browning did not correct his mistake until the revised edition where the "clear cackle is easily uttered" (l. 570). Ironically, Alfred Austin had in *My Satire and Its Censors* presented critics as geese that quacked. Austin portrays the critics as being addressed by their bosses as follows:

Wake, snoring scribes! Ye varlets! do ye hear?
Up from your straw each drowsy garreteer!
. . . .
Extend your neck, each interrupted goose,
And quack me quick five shillings' of abuse.[37]

Did Browning at first mean to allude to Austin? If he did, had he forgotten that intention by 1889 when he revised the poem? I think not. But I think he did recall the criticism put forth by the *Saturday Review* in 1876: "Mr. Browning, in his dreary and laboured jocosity, has apparently confounded geese with ducks."[38] It is ironic indeed that Browning would appear to take into account the quibbling of the critics in revising a poem about how he has no intention of taking into account the quibbling of the critics.

It is apparent that throughout all the stages of "Pacchiarotto and How He Worked in Distemper," Browning revised carefully and thoughtfully to improve his poem. It would not seem that Browning was in a state of mental agitation when he prepared the poem for publication. He did not operate under the compulsion to release long-pent-up resentments regardless of how he expressed them. The thoughtful manner of Browning's revisions, rather, suggests a poet out to have a bit of sport knocking about those who had done the same to him. His success, as always, depended upon the skill and care of his execution and so required that he indeed work in good temper.

NOTES

1. Review in *Saturday Review* 42 (August 12, 1876): 205.

2. Review in *Graphic* 14 (Sept. 9, 1876): 254, 255. The latter quotation was preceded by the following remark: "What a comfortable frame of mind it must be when a poet entertains a perfect belief of his own wisdom and excellence, and an utter contempt for other folks' opinion!" (p. 254).

3. Edward Berdow, *Browning Cyclopaedia*, 8th ed. (London: George Allen and Unwin, 1916), p. 307.

4. William Lyon Phelps, "Robert Browning and Alfred Austin," *Yale Review* 7 (April 1918): 590.

5. Norton B. Crowell, *Alfred Austin: Victorian* (Albuquerque: University of New Mexico Press, 1953), pp. 110, 116.

6. William Irvine and Park Honan, *The Book, the Ring, and the Poet: A New Biography of Robert Browning* (New York: McGraw-Hill, 1974), p. 483. Boyd Litzinger and Donald Smalley call "Pacchiarotto" "ill-natured and more diatribe than poetry" (Introduction to *Browning: The Critical Heritage* [London: Routledge & Kegan Paul, 1970], p. 21). Browning did think Alfred Austin, the chief target of the poem, "a filthy little snob," as he puts it to his confidante, Isa Blagden (Letter of 22 March 1870, in *Dearest Isa: Robert Browning's Letters to Isabella Blagden*, ed. Edward C. McAleer [Austin: University of Texas Press, 1951], p. 332).

7. Clyde de L. Ryals, *Browning's Later Poetry, 1871–1889* (Ithaca, N.Y.: Cornell University Press, 1975), p. 135. For an example of a poet responding to his critics in a genuinely angry manner, see Wordsworth's "Essay, Supplementary to the

Preface" wherein he finds "critics too petulant to be passive to a genuine poet, and too feeble to grapple with him; men, who take upon them to report of the course which *he* holds whom they are utterly unable to accompany,—confounded if he turn quick upon the wing, dismayed if he soar steadily 'into the region;'—men of palsied imaginations and indurated hearts; in whose minds all healthy action is languid, who therefore feed as the many direct them, or, with the many, are greedy after vicious provocatives;—judges, whose censure is auspicious, and whose praise ominous!" (*The Prose Works of William Wordsworth*, ed. W. J. B. Owen and Jane Worthington Smyser [Oxford: Clarendon Press, 1974], 3:66).

8. Neither the manuscript, first edition, nor revised edition contains line numbers. I have numbered the lines according to the revised edition, and these line numbers serve as reference points when I cite earlier versions of the poem.

9. The complete manuscript of *Pacchiarotto and How He Worked in Distemper: with Other Poems* is in Balliol College Library and is bound with *La Saisiaz* and *The Two Poets of Croisic* (1878) in brown morocco, with the Browning family coat of arms stamped in gold on the front cover. The poems together are catalogued as Balliol MS 390.

10. The last page of the manuscript contains the marked-out note that Browning began to write on 15 April 1876 and that he finished on 1 May 1876. The dates are preceded by the abbreviation L. D. I. E., also marked out. L. D. I. E. = *Laus Deo in excelsis*.

11. The location of proofs for this poem is unknown (Philip Kelley and Betty A. Coley, comps., *The Browning Collections: A Reconstruction with Other Memorabilia* [Waco, Tex.; New York; Winfield, Kan.; and London: Armstrong Browning Library, The Browning Institute, Wedgestone Press, and Mansell, 1983], p. 39). All of my references to revisions of the proofs are assumptions about proof-revision based on differences between the MS and the first edition.

The first edition was published on 18 July 1876 by Smith, Elder Co. The 241 pages plus title and "contents" pages of the octavo volume were bound in boards of drab cloth. It sold for seven shillings six pence, and 2,500 copies were printed. A full bibliographical description of the 1876 edition is provided in Leslie N. Broughton, Clark S. Northup, and Robert Pearsall, *Robert Browning: A Bibliography, 1830–1950* (Ithaca, N.Y.: Cornell University Press, 1953), p. 19.

Pacchiarotto and How He Worked in Distemper: with Other Poems is in volume fourteen of the 1888–89 final edition of *Poetical Works*, together with *La Saisiaz* and *The Two Poets of Croisic*. There are 279 pages plus title and "contents" pages of the volume, which is bound in brown cloth boards. See Broughton, Northup, and Pearsall, p. 36.

12. On the manuscript, Browning mistakenly repeated the number 14, throwing off the numbering of this and the subsequent sections. This error was corrected in the first edition.

13. The third line here originally read "Who shieldest the fault of the [word illegible]."

14. E. A. Horsman, ed., *The Diary of Alfred Domett, 1820–1885* (Oxford: Oxford University Press, 1953), p. 149.

15. The following from Austin's *The Poetry of the Period* ([London: Richard Bentley, 1870], pp. 75f) will make Browning's attitude toward Austin understandable:

> To Mr. Tennyson's credit be it spoken, he has never gone looking for fame. The ground we tread on is delicate; and I will, therefore, only add that one should have been better pleased if the author, who is now so ridiculously obtruded as his rival, had imitated him in that particular. Small London literary coteries, and large London salons, cannot crown a man with the bays of Apollo. They may stick their trumpery tinsel wreath upon him, but these will last no longer than the locks they encircle. They may confer notoriety, but fame is not in their gift. Let the sane general public therefore, I say, take heart, and bluntly forswear Mr. Browning and all his works. It is bad enough that there should be people, pretending to authority among us, who call a man a great poet when, though unquestionably a poet, he has no marks of greatness about him. But that is a venial error, and a trifling misfortune compared to what would be the misery in an age which gibbeted itself beforehand for the pity of posterity, by deliberately calling a man a poet who—however remarkable his mental attributes and powers—is not specifically a poet at all. I hope we shall be spared this humiliation. At any rate, I must protest against being supposed willingly to participate in it.

16. Later changed to "drabs"; see p. 122.

17. W. J. Turner, *Beethoven: The Search for Reality* (New York: George H. Doran, 1927), pp. 246–47, remarks on Beethoven's having "more affinity . . . with Donne than Spenser, . . . with Browning than Tennyson."

18. Review of *Aristophanes' Apology*, *Pall Mall Gazette* 22 (15 July 1875): 203–4. This quotation was pointed out by Kenneth L. Knickerbocker.

19. In revising the proofs, Browning removed the question mark in the second line, making the second statement answer to the question in l. 492.

20. Lord Byron, of course, had established the precedent of identifying critics as diminutive, referring in "English Bards and Scotch Reviews" to the critic's pen as "that mighty instrument of little men!" (l. 10) (William H. Marshall, ed., *Selected Poems and Letters* [New York: New York University Press, 1977], p. 7).

21. Phelps, p. 585, mistakenly points out that "the Greek word *skoramis* was . . . an afterthought, and must have been substituted during the reading of the proof." Actually the only changes the poet made for this passage during the proofreading were to add an exclamation point following *march* (replacing a comma), a comma following *housemaid*, and a dash after *hand* (replacing the two-dot ellipsis).

22. "Pacchiarotto" is written in the style of Austin's *My Satire and Its Censors* (London: George Manwaring, 1861), which is a "vitriolic diatribe" against William Hepworth Dixon, editor of the *Athenaeum* (1853–69) and responsible for

much adverse criticism of Austin himself. Austin is much more precise, relentless, and personal in his attack on his chief detractor than Browning is on Austin (see Crowell, pp. 55–62). In "Pacchiarotto" Browning takes up the couplet with the occasional triplet employed by Austin in *My Satire* (see p. 9 where Austin rhymes *ulcerate*, *state*, and *prate*) and exaggerates the style, employing the triplet much more frequently.

23. Cf. Austin:

> Propriety and printers' devils call:
> Pluck your own quill and plunge it in your gall.
> (p. 10)

24. The second line was not arrived at without a false start. The first edition concludes l. 537 with an exclamation mark.

25. In revising for the first edition Browning changed the final line here to "Of their charms—how are most frank, how few venal!"

26. And at the same time he omitted the unnecessary (for the sense) and metrically superfluous "was."

27. For the first edition Browning hyphenated "wall-sides" and combined "wherewith" as one word. Another example of Browning's clarifying what is done in an interior setting is found in ll. 170–71: originally he wrote, "Hop, skip, jump, from room's inside," which he revised and expanded as follows: "Hop, skip, jump, to inside from outside / of chamber."

28. A few lines later, when Pacchiarotto is described as approaching the rostrum to address these "Free Horses," we observe Browning following his usual approach to revision and then subsequently backing off. The narrator originally said that the painter "stepped forth, mounted rostrum." Wanting to express the speed with which Pacchiarotto did this, Browning made two significant changes; Pacchiarotto now "sprang forth, rushed to rostrum." Realizing that both of these changes exceeded effectiveness, Browning retreated during the proofreading and restored "mounted" (l. 247).

29. Browning gave punctuation commensurate with the forceful expression when he revised the proofs, ending the line with an exclamation mark.

30. Browning's first try on the manuscript was "Pace back and forward, friend / Of those what explore its four corners?"

31. A clog is a "block or heavy piece of wood . . . attached to the leg or neck of a man or beast, to impede motion or prevent escape" (*OED*, sense 2), and the fetlock is that "part of a horse's leg where the tuft of hair grows behind the pastern-joint" (*OED*, sense 1).

32. *Saturday Review*, p. 205; W. C. DeVane, *A Browning Handbook*, 2d ed. (New York: Appleton-Century-Crofts, 1955), p. 395.

33. The *OED* cites Dicken's *Nicholas Nickleby* wherein he describes "old gentlemen in drabs and gaiters."

34. See Ashby Bland Crowder, "Stages in the Composition of *The Inn Album*," *Browning Institute Studies* 5 (1977): 67.

35. Crowder, p. 67.

36. DeVane, p. 394.
37. Austin, pp. 10, 11.
38. *Saturday Review,* p. 205. It is worth noting that Browning's revisions did disregard the *Saturday Review's* observation that he had made a subject-verb agreement error in *The Inn Album,* even though Domett's *Diary* records Browning's reaction to the error's being pointed out. See review of *The Inn Album, Saturday Review* 30 (4 December 1875): 716; and Horsman, p. 162.

8

Approaching Truth "on One Side after Another": Revision in the Religious Prose of Matthew Arnold

Suzanne O. Edwards

Matthew Arnold was often criticized by his readers for the arrogant, dogmatic tone of his prose. Responding to such a charge from his sister, Jane, who had accused him of "becoming as dogmatic as Ruskin," Arnold told her, "the difference was that Ruskin was dogmatic and *wrong*." (*Letters* 1:200).[1] Such a flippant reply would suggest that Arnold was so sure of his opinions that he would believe reconsideration of his arguments unnecessary. On the contrary, for Arnold, each act of prose composition entailed a "re-vision" of what he had written before, a reevaluation frequently prompted by critical reaction to his ideas or presentation of them. As Sidney Coulling and Robert Super have demonstrated, on more than one occasion Arnold planned a brief essay or lecture that would present his position on an issue only to find several more essays or lectures required to answer his critics' objections or clarify his views.[2] Arnold's expansive essay sequences reveal his responsiveness to his audience and his practice of reviewing previous compositions at virtually every opportunity.

While Arnold made extensive revisions in the sense of modifying punctuation, altering diction, and recasting sentences, he was not merely interested in surface features such as these. Neither did his reappraisal of what he had written often lead to concessions or altered theories. Rather, Arnold sought in new works to clarify through elaboration and extension arguments he had already presented but which his readers had somehow misunderstood.

To establish this pattern, I will analyze several of the prose works Arnold wanted most to be remembered for—namely, his essays on religion. While Arnold wrote about religion from 1862 until his death in 1888, this paper will focus on the four great religious books he published in the 1870s. My intention is not to debate the validity of Arnold's views or fix their place in the history of religious exegesis, nor do I attempt to assess the soundness of his rhetoric.[3] Rather my aim is to demonstrate the evolution of his argument from its early expression in *St. Paul and Protestantism* through successive revisions to his most mature presentation of it in *Last Essays on Church and Religion.*

Arnold's four major religious works were serialized in popular journals and later published in book form, sometimes running into several editions. Each periodical installment allowed Arnold the opportunity to reshape and strengthen the argument he had set forth in earlier essays that had already attracted public attention and criticism. A similar opportunity to expand and also a chance to reorganize were afforded when a sequence of essays was collected and printed in a book-length edition. Moreover, each new work grew out of those previously published.[4] In the first, *St. Paul and Protestantism* (1870), Arnold notes that biblical interpretation will not be a new project for him but merely a continuation—or as he confidently and optimistically proclaims—a *completion* of what he has "already begun" in the fifth chapter of *Culture and Anarchy* (1869) entitled "Porro Unum Est Necessarium" (6:7). However, further development of Arnold's position proved necessary and appeared as *Literature and Dogma* (1873), a book which provoked such controversy that he conceived the notion of presenting "a review of objections" to it in another volume, *God and the Bible* (1875). Still he was not finished with the subject. Two years later Arnold published his *Last Essays on Church and Religion,* four essays that do not so much offer new ideas as they do Arnold's last extended discourse on a subject with which he had long been preoccupied. Two central aims predominate in these four books: to save the Church from the dissolution threatened by scientific inquiry and to persuade Englishmen of the need for a unified national church. These theses are discussed in *St. Paul and Protestantism* and reviewed in three subsequent works. An analysis of the four will review how Arnold adhered to his original propositions while altering his manner of presenting them.

Arnold's attention to the subject of religion derives, as a matter of course, from his abiding concern for cultural progress, by which he means both intellectual and spiritual growth. By promoting a general critical attitude, culture aims "to make reason and the will of God prevail," he tells us in *Culture and Anarchy* (Arnold's quote from Bishop Wilson 5:91). The critical approach, then, must apply to religious issues as well as to political and aesthetic ones. Arnold is convinced that England's middle classes, the Philistines, are especially lacking in culture largely because of their self-satisfied complacency and their unwillingness to examine religious convictions objectively and dispassionately. From Arnold's perspective, the purpose of religion is the same as the purpose of that broader culture to which it contributes: both aim for "human perfection" (5:93). And perfection is something one moves *toward,* he explains in *Culture and Anarchy:* "Not a having and a resting, but a growing and a becoming, is the character of perfection as culture conceives it; and here, too, it coincides with religion" (5:94). Instead of being satisfied to approach the Bible and the Church critically, to move *toward* enlightenment and spiritual perfection, members of the middle class seem drawn to dissenting sects that discourage questioning and prescribe complex dogma.

As Ruth apRoberts explains, such dogmatism is anathema to Arnold.[5] Though his opponents (and his sister Jane) might disagree, Arnold certainly never saw himself as doctrinaire. He describes his own tentative, exploratory method of inquiry in the preface to the first edition of *Essays and Criticism* (1865):

> Indeed, it is not in my nature,—some of my critics would rather say, not in my power,—to dispute on behalf of any opinion, even my own, very obstinately. To try and approach truth on one side after another, not to strive or cry, not to persist in pressing forward, on any one side, with violence and self-will,—it is only thus, it seems to me, that mortals may hope to gain any vision of the mysterious Goddess, whom we shall never meet except in outline, but only thus even in outline. He who will do nothing but fight impetuously toward her on his own, one, favourite, particular line, is inevitably destined to run his head into the folds of the black robe in which she is wrapped. (3:286)

Arnold's religious prose illustrates his ongoing search for truth "on one side after another."

All of Arnold's works result from his compulsion to liberate the masses, to teach them, as it were, how to read. By modeling for them the open-minded, critical approach he espouses, he hopes to persuade them to reexamine their convictions and the basis for them. Writing to his mother after the second part of *St. Paul and Protestantism* appeared in the *Cornhill* in November 1869, Arnold declares, "Whether I have rendered St. Paul's ideas with perfect correctness or not, there is no doubt that the confidence with which these people [middle class Nonconformists] regarded their conventional rendering of them was quite baseless, made them narrow and intolerant, and prevented all progress" (*Letters* 2:21).

In *St. Paul and Protestantism,* Arnold is anxious "to rescue St. Paul and the Bible from the perversions of them by mistaken men" (6:7). He wants to recover the essence of Paul's message from the distortions of it by close-minded Dissenters in order to reinstate the experiential basis of biblical wisdom. Misreading the Bible, Arnold reasons, contributes to both the prospective dissolution and the perpetual disunity of the Church. Therefore, Arnold repeatedly warns against naive, literal readings of the Bible as well as reductive scientific interpretations. Since

Protestantism is so closely identified with Pauline doctrine, says Arnold, it is essential that Paul's "fundamental ideas [be] disengaged from the elaborate misconceptions with which Protestantism has overlaid them" in order that they may "have an influence in the future greater than any which they have yet had" (6:5).

From Arnold's perspective it is the Nonconformists—Calvinists and Methodists, for instance—who have been particularly prone to misinterpret St. Paul. Determination to substantiate established views had made it impossible for such biased churchmen to "turn a free and fresh stream of thought upon the whole matter" of religion and "see things as they really are" (5:235, 252). Arnold proposes to compare what St. Paul actually wrote to the Puritan theology supposedly based on his writings. He reminds his readers of the distinction he made in *Culture and Anarchy* between Hebraism and Hellenism and of his application of this distinction to religion: "we were led to remark how the over-Hebraising of Puritanism, and its want of a wide culture, do so narrow its range and impair its vision that even the documents which it thinks all-sufficient . . . it does not rightly understand, but is apt to make of them something quite different from what they really are" (6:7). At this point, Arnold quotes himself, a rhetorical strategy he employs often, signifying as do his frequent allusions to his own essays, the recursive nature of his process of composition.[6] "In short, no man, we said, who knows nothing else, knows even his Bible." He continues, "And we showed how readers of the Bible attached to essential words and ideas of the Bible a sense which was not the writer's" (6:7). Convinced of the soundness of his previous statements, pleased in many instances with the very wording he previously employed, Arnold repeats himself. But the very fact that he has taken up his pen again testifies to his awareness of the need for revision through additional substantiation of his cherished phrases. And this is what he offers. In *Culture and Anarchy* Arnold's concern is with culture as a whole and only with religion to the extent (a major one from his perspective) that it contributes to or serves as an agent of the larger culture. In *St. Paul and Protestantism* religion becomes the central focus.

Arnold's tone in these pages is patient and indulgent. Although, he seems to say, he has already clearly demonstrated the waywardness of the Hebraistic tendency in *Culture and Anarchy,* since some remain unconvinced, he will "take the present opportunity of going further in the same road" (6:7). As it turns out "the same road" continues for another 125 pages. Perhaps as the reader takes this journey with him, he will come to see things as he ought. And Arnold counts on the reader's willingness to accompany him. After all, surely Nonconformists want the truth of Pauline doctrine revealed: "Puritanism certainly wished well to St. Paul; it cannot wish to compromise him by an unintelligent adhesion to him and a blind adoption of his words, instead of being a true child to him" (6:8). Arnold, therefore, will simultaneously demonstrate the validity of his denunciation of narrow-minded, excessive Hebraising and the value of the disinterested, critical inquiry he advocates by applying the method of culture to a detailed reading of St. Paul.

Arnold contends that a "critical" reading of St. Paul shows "what in St. Paul is secondary and subordinate, Puritanism has made primary and essential" (6:8). Arnold is thinking specifically of the Calvinist doctrine of election and the Methodist doctrine of salvation through faith. In making God active and man passive, in stressing "what God does, with disregard to what man does" (6:17), such dogma runs counter to the teachings of Paul who focused on man's experience of righteousness. Arnold sees Puritans as content *"to rest in the finished work of the Saviour"* (Arnold's italics, 6:46). Paul, on the other hand, argued that identification with Christ will make a difference in man's everyday existence. The active Christian will sacrifice as Christ did; he will die to his own sins and temptations as Christ did (6:47).

Misreading has resulted from naive literalism, from a failure to apply the method of culture. Because they ignore the poetic, or metaphorical, quality of biblical language, the Nonconformists draw erroneous conclusions. Arnold maintains, "what in St. Paul is figure and belongs to the sphere of feeling, Puritanism has transported into the sphere of intellect and made thesis and formula" (6:8). Often Paul spoke figuratively or rhetorically, yet his writings have been taken verbatim by those determined to justify "preconceived theories" (6:20). To further complicate matters, Arnold warns, Paul himself was guilty of using scriptures in an "arbitrary and uncritical fashion, as if they had a talismanic character" (6:22). Rather than transcribing Paul's words literally, a modern reader's only recourse is to deconstruct Paul's meaning, or in Arnold's words, "to translate" Paul's intentions (6:23). For example, says Arnold, while Paul firmly believed in the resurrection of Christ "in the physical and miraculous sense," he also thought of resurrection in symbolic terms (6:51). For Paul, living in sin brings spiritual death; one lives when he follows Jesus and rejects sin. Arnold argues that most importantly, though not exclusively, "the resurrection Paul was striving after for himself and others was a resurrection *now,* and a resurrection to *righteousness*" (6:52). In Arnold's opinion, St. Paul's contribution as a religious teacher surfaces in his "effort to find a moral side and significance for all the processes, however mystical, of the religious life, with a view of strengthening, in this way, their hold upon us and their command of all our nature" (6:51). We must read with this in mind. To arrive at an intelligent understanding of Paul's message, we must approach his texts as we would those of any other author—thoughtfully and critically.

The final installment of *St. Paul and Protestantism* reveals Arnold's sensitivity to his readers' responses. Accused of presumptuousness in presenting his "translation" as *the* right one, Arnold wrote a fourth essay entitled "Modern Dissent." This piece served as the preface for the original publication of *St. Paul and Protestantism* in book form in May 1870, but Arnold shifted it to the end of the volume for the 1887 and subsequent editions when his readers complained that the book was written "backwards" (6:229). In "Modern Dissent" Arnold answers the criticism already voiced by readers of the three-part serial version by insisting that the views he has presented are neither novel nor idiosyncratic. His interpretation of St. Paul is simply a reflection of the Zeitgeist, the spirit of the times (6:111). Throughout his poetry and prose Arnold addresses this issue of the temper of the times and repeatedly comments on the dilemma of modern man, born into an atmosphere of uncertainty, doubt, and confusion. Traditional sources of authority such as the Church are diminishing. For those "wandering between two worlds, one dead, / The other powerless to be born," questioning is inevitable. And the answers—to whatever extent answers are possible—must be ones that modern, scientific man can accept, be sustained by, and find comfort in.

Besides, unlike the Puritans who claim to render spiritual truth, *the* Gospel, Arnold readily acknowledges that his "conception" of St. Paul's writings is an evolving one that tends toward truth (6:111–12). Since Arnold has proclaimed elsewhere that a movement *toward* truth and understanding is the very aim that culture can realistically expect to fulfill, it comes as no surprise that he makes such an admission. Human beings are not capable of comprehending God all at once, but they are capable through open-minded inquiry of coming closer to truth than the Puritans have with their unyielding dogmatism. Arnold admits that his interpretation of St. Paul may be flawed, but he is certain it has more validity because of its disinterestedness, than the provincial readings of the Nonconformists. Arnold closes by conceding that it may not be possible to realize his aims in the near future: "To disengage the religion of England from unscriptural Protestantism, political Dissent, and a spirit of watchful jealousy, may be an aim not in our day reachable; and still it is well to level at it" (6:127). In fact, Arnold continued to level at such disengagement by writing *Literature and Dogma*.

Ruth apRoberts points out that in *Literature and Dogma* Arnold extends his critical approach to reading St. Paul "to the Bible as a whole and to religion in general" (189). Arnold's views have not changed. He does not revoke prior arguments; he repeats them. And while *Literature and Dogma* is more than twice as long as *St. Paul and Protestantism*, Arnold does not actually introduce new ideas. Instead he expands those previously advanced by broadening their application. Moreover, Arnold demonstrates more impressively than ever before his familiarity with the Bible and with biblical criticism, thereby strengthening his position among the ranks of those religious commentators who merit the public's serious attention.

Arnold's title for his second major religious book signifies once again his belief that the Bible is a powerful work of literature and should be read as such. As a literary work, it must be approached from the method of culture—an objective critical inquiry founded on a broad-based knowledge of philosophy, literature, history. Arnold patiently reminds his readers he has made the same recommendation repeatedly in the past. By "acquainting ourselves with the best that has been known and said in the world, and thus with the history of the human spirit," we are more likely "to put the right construction on the Bible" (6:151). We substitute for abstract "unverifiable assumptions" the "real experimental basis" of the Bible, making it possible for the Bible to "reach the people" (6:151). Since Arnold sees the Bible as "the Book of *conduct*" (6:408) and he calculates conduct to be "three-fourths of life" (6:175), he considers it crucial that readers come as close to "the right construction" as possible.

Arnold remains convinced that an acceptance "that the language of the Bible is fluid, passing, and literary, not rigid, fixed, and scientific, is the first step towards a right understanding of the Bible" (6:152). Consequently, he begins *Literature and Dogma* by reiterating the contention of *St. Paul and Protestantism* that theologians have wrongfully treated figurative, poetic terms from the Bible as if they were factual, scientific terms. Arnold maintains that attempts to eliminate or explain away all inconsistencies and improbabilities from scriptural interpretation are unnecessary once one accepts that the Bible has little value as theological discourse. The significance and the beauty of the Bible lie in its power to engage the feelings of readers and thus inspire noble conduct. "The true meaning of religion," says Arnold, is *"morality touched by emotion"* (Arnold's italics, 6:176). Men and women respond more forcefully to songs, stories, and parables that relate to their experience, stir their imagination, and touch their emotions than they do to abstract theories or dry scientific analysis. Yet within the Church, conduct has been less stressed than creed. And Arnold finds this emphasis most regrettable, since the subject of religion is not theories about the nature of God. The practical purpose of religion and its chief value as a cultural force, Arnold points out, have been to cause man to care about conduct, to commit himself to righteousness. This the Bible as a work of literature achieves. Thus Arnold responds to his readers' charges of the sacrilege inherent in his approach to scripture by demonstrating that the Bible's literary character supplies its strength, not its weakness.

Arnold recognizes the dilemma of applying the critical approach he proposes to reading scripture which "we have been trained to regard . . . as a sort of talisman given down to us out of Heaven" (6:159). Yet difficult as we may find the disinterested method of culture, it is essential. "For, after all, the Bible is *not* a talisman, to be taken and used literally; neither is any existing Church a talisman, whatever pretensions of the sort it may make, for giving the right interpretation of the Bible. Only true culture can give us this interpretation" (6:162). And Arnold argues as he did in the "Preface" to *Culture and Anarchy*, "culture is *reading*; but reading with a purpose to guide it, and with system. He does a good work who does anything to help this; indeed, it is the one essential service now to be rendered to education" (6:162).[7] Therefore, if we will allow it, he will endeavor once more to model the critical method, to direct our reading, to perform the "essential service" of educating us.

In chapter one, Arnold addresses more specifically the problem of decoding or translating biblical language. Even the appellation *God*, he says, is a literary term that has different meanings for different people (6:171). It cannot justifiably be presented as a scientific designation with a precise definition. Instead, Arnold elects to describe God as "the *not ourselves* which makes for righteousness" (6:189). As W. David Shaw puts it, this vague definition offers "peace to his soul without insulting his intelligence" (127), and he expects it to do the same for his readers. Arnold willingly admits the inadequacy of such a definition, but it expresses, in his opinion, all that can be known for certain. And, he hastens to reassure the reader, an acceptance of the limitations of human knowledge about the nature of God need not destroy faith. Although he doubts human ability to identify conclusively the true nature of God, Arnold does not doubt and never denies the existence of God.

In *St. Paul and Protestantism,* when he elects to focus on the writings of one religious teacher, Paul, Arnold contents himself with identifying God "scientifically" as the *"stream of tendency by which all things seek to fulfil the law of their being"* (6:10), or put in simpler terms, he presents God as that which inspires individuals to do good. In *Literature and Dogma* his subject has broadened to include the entire Bible. Since "in the Bible God is everything" (as he will later say in *God and the Bible* 7:156), Arnold must now explain his idea of God more fully. He maintains that God's existence is revealed—not by such tangible evidence as that found in the physical world but by man's conscience which is his guide to God's law. He reasons, "To please God, to serve God, to obey God's will, means to follow a law of things which is found in conscience, and which is an indication, irrespective of our arbitrary wish and fancy, of what we ought to do. There *is,* then, a real power which makes for righteousness; and it is the greatest of realities for us" (6:190). All human experience proves that God exists.

But Christians have not been satisfied with the simple experiential proof of the existence of God. To convince his readers of a need to deconstruct biblical language, to arrive at the simple truth of God's message, Arnold attempts to show how embellishments were added. Over the centuries a number of "extra beliefs" have been imposed on Christianity with the result that personal morality has been overshadowed (6:231). Man has rested his faith on reports of the supposed fulfillment of divine prophecy and the performance of miracles. Extra belief in and of itself is not harmful, Arnold maintains, and may even be beneficial if it inspires man to improve his conduct. This was quite likely in the past when the masses more willingly accepted church teachings without question. However, nineteenth-century churchgoers, afflicted by doubt and confusion, are not so easily swayed. Arnold fears that when, inevitably, the temper of the times influences the modern believer to distrust the literal truth of his extra belief, he may extend his misgivings to all of religion and find "the basis of conduct gone" (6:232). This need not happen. For as Dorothea Krook puts it, Arnold aims to convince his audience that "the miraculous foundation of historic Christianity" is "*irrelevant* to the internal experimental truth of Christ's gospel" (my emphasis, 211).

As he does in *Culture and Anarchy,* Arnold credits the ancient Hebrews with finding "the revelation needed to breathe emotion into the laws of morality, and to make morality religion"; however, "this revelation lost, as time went on, its nearness and clearness" (6:215). Religion for the people of Israel became a public concern, "a matter of national and social duties mainly," not a deeply felt individual commitment (6:215). By serving as a model for Christians to follow, Jesus reinstated *"personal religion"* (6:217). "Self-examination [what Arnold elsewhere refers to as "inwardness"], self-renouncement, and mildness, were, therefore, the great means by which Jesus Christ renewed righteousness and religion" (6:220–21). Only personal religion is strong enough to guide conduct, and personal religion need not depend upon belief in miracles. For the spiritual genius of Jesus resides in the "power of his *words,*" not in his questionable performance of miracles (6:254).

Arnold cautions us to remember that Jesus himself does not report his miracles. They are recounted by his followers, superstitious men predisposed to see "thaumaturgy in all that Jesus did"; lesser, fallible men, moreover, who "could err and did err" (6:255, 250). Arnold here extends to all the Bible writers the disclaimers he attached to St. Paul, saying for example of the New Testament writers that they "speak about Jesus and give a priceless record of him, without adequately and accurately comprehending him. They are altogether on another plane from Jesus, and their mistakes are not his" (6:258). Again, we must think of them as authors and of the Bible as a work of literature. We are safest in accepting the more direct teachings of Jesus—his parables and single-sentence maxims. While such moral pronouncements may be reported out of context, they are probably for the most part accurate since they would be easy to remember and record faithfully (6:270). In any event, they are as we have seen more central to Christ's purpose than any miracles he might have performed since they teach man how to live.

Predictably, Arnold can no more be sure of the meaning of the name "Christ" than he can be of the name "God." But, he claims, this uncertainty should pose no great barrier to the reader of the Bible. Even though we cannot verify whether Jesus was literally the son of God, Arnold has no doubt that Jesus was the "offspring," or the product, of the power that makes for righteousness, and this suffices for him (6:375). Unfortunately over the years, "Christianity developed more and more its side of miracle and legend; until to believe Jesus to be the Son of God meant to believe the points of the legend,—his preternatural conception of birth, his miracles, his descent into hell, his bodily resurrection, his ascent into heaven, and his future triumphant return to judgment" (6:340).

What Arnold labels the *"popular science* of Christianity" has become sanctified by Church dogma and now substitutes for true spirituality (6:340). Jesus himself did not deal with theory, "with what are called Church matters at all"; he dealt with experience (6:344). From Arnold's vantage point, all doctrine presents "a false criticism of the Bible, an *illusion"* because, as he has said before, it all "assumes what cannot be *verified"* and distracts man's attention from what is truly important—conduct (6:355, 361). Sadly, the Church has drifted far from the original aims of Christ. Arnold disdains revealed religion, asking, "Walking on the water, multiplying loaves, raising corpses, a heavenly judge appearing with trumpets in the clouds while we are yet alive,—what is this compared to the real experience offered as witness to us by Christianity? It is like the difference between the grandeur of an extravaganza and the grandeur of the sea or the sky" (6:400).

He maintains that faith does not depend on "supernatural prescience" or miracle (6:233). "Faith is: *the being able to cleave to a power of goodness appealing to our higher and real self, not to our lower and apparent self"* (6:315). Arnold concludes, "The more we trace the real law of Christianity's action the grander it will seem" (6:400).

In his closing Arnold explicitly relates *Literature and Dogma* to his earlier works. By claiming that conduct is three-fourths of life, he has not contradicted the emphasis he placed on culture in works such as *Culture and Anarchy*. Culture serves "the interest of religion" by preventing "our mis-handling and sophisticating" religious issues and texts (6:409). Despite this assurance, "mishandling" was precisely what many of Arnold's readers found him guilty of. In a letter of 21 September 1874 to the editor of the *Contemporary Review*, James Knowles, Arnold identifies two "main objections" raised against *Literature and Dogma:* his "refusal to affirm a personal God" and his "use of the Fourth Gospel" (quoted in Coulling 238).

Confident of the merits of his argument, he began to compose an extended defense. Writing to his sister Frances on 2 October 1874 Arnold declares, "It will more and more become evident how entirely religious is the work I have done in *Literature and Dogma*." He recognizes that this will take time but is determined to persist, telling his sister in the same letter, "no one knows better than I do how little of a popular author I am; but the thing is, I gradually produce a real effect, and the public acquires a kind of obscure interest in me as this gets to be perceived" (*Letters* 2:117). Hoping to capitalize on the public interest he had already aroused and prove the "entirely religious" nature of his biblical criticism, Arnold published in the *Contemporary Review* from October 1874 to September 1875 a series of seven essays intended to counter the opposition to his controversial book. The original title of the sequence, "Review of Objections to *Literature and Dogma*," proclaims his intention. While R. H. Super rightly notes that this title does the essays an "injustice" (7:439), it reveals Arnold's view of the work as another installment in his ongoing dialectic with his readers. Arnold settled on the title *God and the Bible* when the essays were collected and published as a book in 1875. The journal title he retained as a subtitle until the 1884 edition, when the subtitle became "A Sequel to *Literature and Dogma*," a similarly significant and more accurate label.

Although *Literature and Dogma* has been labeled "anti-christian and anti-religious" by his opponents, Arnold says at the outset that he does not mean to strike with "hard words in return" (7:142). But he is quick to insist that he has no thought of altering his position either. He remains as opposed as ever to theology which presents no more than a "grotesque mixture . . . of learned pseudo-science with popular legend" and goes so far as to proclaim that it is the proponents of popular religion and the learned theologians "who in our judgment owe an apology to Christianity and to religion, not we" (7:142).

Putting aside the angry attacks of the narrow-minded and fanatical as scarcely worthy of his notice, he turns his attention to intelligent, reasonable criticisms which do deserve a reply. His "object" has consistently been "to find sure and safe grounds for the continued use and authority of the Bible" (7:146). Many, no longer able to accept the Bible as literal truth, were taught in *Literature and Dogma* a more profitable way of interpreting scripture, he claims. Arnold worries that these individuals to whom he has been "of service" may be "puzzled and shaken by some of the objections" that have been raised to his book. He fears they may lose the "sure hold on the Bible" he has helped them establish and will find themselves "more and more baffled, distressed, and bewildered in their dealings with religion" (7:150). Repeatedly in *God and the Bible* Arnold addresses this select audience directly ("the reader of *Literature and Dogma* will recollect," "those in whose interest *Literature and Dogma* was written," "the readers of *Literature and Dogma* who had taken our advice and had begun to find profit from it," [7:163, 166, 199]) and continually renews his commitment to making the Bible accessible to them.

Arnold begins by reviewing his accomplishments in *Literature and Dogma*. First he required the reader of the Bible "to face that primary question . . . what 'God' means in the Bible, and to see that it means the Eternal not ourselves that makes for righteousness." Second, he caused the reader to "ask himself what is meant by . . . 'knowing Christ' . . . and find that it means laying hold of the method and secret and temper of Jesus" (7:157). Having recalled to the readers' attention these now familiar propositions, he sets out to verify them. In the first three installments, he defends his definition of God and his inability to grant the occurrence of miracles. Meeting the opposition to his unwillingness to profess belief in a personal God, Arnold reminds his readers that he has not denied the existence of a personal God; he has only said that the reality of a personal God cannot be proven (7:160–61). In response to the criticism that he slighted the subject of miracles by treating it so briefly, Arnold justifies having done so because the important issue is not whether miracles can be believed but rather "what becomes of religion,—so precious, as we believe, to the human race,—if miracles cannot be relied on?" (7:164). Arnold admits he has been led to "dismiss with tenderness" a belief in miracles. "One abandons them with a kind of unwilling disenchantment, and only because one must," he says (7:199). But "the metaphysics of learned theology" one can dismiss with "sheer satisfaction" as something no one ever understood or enjoyed (7:198, 199). Neither is necessary for the Christian faith. Arnold advises the reader to ignore both the "assailants" of the Bible and the "apologists" for it (7:172) and to pursue his own critical inquiry.

In four subsequent articles, Arnold scrutinizes the current debate about the biblical canon and the reliability of "Bible-testimony," especially that rendered in the Fourth Gospel (7:240). Arnold sees in the Book of John much evidence of "the genuine teaching of Jesus" which gives the account "a peculiar eminency and value" (7:238). However, extremist readings of the Fourth Gospel are adopted both by adherents of popular religion, bent on supporting narrow, orthodox theories, as well as by higher German critics, determined to expose as superstition any belief in the non-natural. Puritans ask no questions and, without hesitation, accept the Bible as literal truth, whereas the German intellectuals mislead by asking too many questions and implying they can all be satisfactorily answered. Arnold sees no need to yield to either extreme. Neither results in the desired effect of helping the individual *"to enjoy the Bible and to turn it to his benefit"* (7:239). Instead, steadily pursuing this frequently stated aim, he feels compelled neither to accept the Book of John as the undisputed word of God nor to dismiss it out of hand. Arnold's solution is to apply the method of literary criticism which he has been teaching us throughout his prose to use. We have applied it to reading St. Paul more intelligently and beneficially; we have applied it with similar results to reading the Bible as a whole; now we will apply it to reading the problematic Johannine Gospel.

For Arnold, the Gospel of John does raise legitimate critical issues about the date of composition and authorship. Though he assumes most of those for whom he is writing have serious misgivings about the credibility of much biblical testimony, it is nonetheless natural, even commendable, for them to be curious and desire further enlightenment, in particular about a book of the Bible that in the nineteenth century was the source of such great controversy. Having thoroughly studied the topic, Arnold offers to save his reader the trouble of working through "the voluminous literature of the subject" (7:244). He requires nothing of his audience but open-mindedness. Remolding comments from "The Function of Criticism at the Present Time" to fit his current audience, he says of his hypothetical reader, "We shall suppose him to come to his inquiry as we did ourselves . . . with the simple desire to see the thing, as far as this may be possible, as it really is" (7:242).

Arnold, as usual, has no intention of changing the statements he has made before; he merely bows to the demand for further substantiation of the ideas he presented in *Literature and Dogma.* As he puts it, he will provide the "grounds" for what he has already said about the Gospels (7:244). His first step is to devote an entire essay to tracing in detail the history of the establishment of the biblical canon. Yet after discussing the matter at length and with considerable show of learning, he arrives at precisely the same conclusion he presented with much less fanfare in *Literature and Dogma.* With the self-satisfied tone of one who has vindicated his own maligned view, he summarizes: "The upshot of all this for the reader of *Literature and Dogma* is, that our original short sentence about the record of the life and words of Jesus holds good. *The record,* we said, *when we first get it, has passed through at least half a century, or more, of oral tradition, and through more than one written account*" (Arnold's italics, 7:271). This exhaustive rehearsal of the textual problems of biblical scholarship would have been unnecessary, he implies, if the accuracy of his claim had not been questioned. Now he has verified his statements; he trusts we are satisfied.

Because of internal inconsistencies and contradictions, Arnold notes that for Liberals "the fashion just now is in favour of theories denying all historical validity to the Fourth Gospel" (7:282). But Arnold insists on examining the historical evidence for himself. His independent, impartial analysis leads him to conjecture that the Apostle John—asked as an old man at Ephesus to share any unrecorded *logia,* or sayings of the Lord, and incidents—relayed them through a Greek Christian, a man entrusted with the sacred task by the Church fathers (7:290). Such an explanation, Arnold maintains, accounts for undeniable peculiarities of style and a foreignness of perspective in the Fourth Gospel. The Book of John conveniently invites Arnold to articulate once more one of his favorite themes. Reconsidering what he has written before and debating how best to strengthen his argument, Arnold sees the Fourth Gospel as supplying him with yet another illustration of the inevitable failings of all Bible writers. "It is the work of a man who, we grant, like all the reporters of Jesus, understood him but imperfectly; who gives us much which is not Jesus, much which comes from himself and his time, much which is addition and legend. But it is the work of a man who gives us this seriously and in good faith" (7:323). Most importantly for Arnold, John contains much that is "genuine" (7:339). We find the writer throughout the Gospel "connecting, repeating, and amplifying themes of Jesus" (7:332).

What Arnold does to recover the essence of John's testament proves necessary in reading any of the Gospels. We cannot read them as "strictly preserved depositions of eye-witnesses" (7:362). No such thing exists. "The exact literary history of our documents is irrecoverable," says Arnold, "and in the absence of it we cannot but have recourse to the test of internal evidence" (7:363). Our concern should not be whether the report of a miracle in the Gospel of John coincides with a report given in the other three Gospels. The writers of the Bible were preoccupied with miracles, but modern Christians have outgrown the need for faith in miracles, have grown embarrassed by them, or soon will (7:367–68). Arnold draws an analogy between "the gradual extinction" during the eighteenth century of a belief in witchcraft and the growing discredit of miracles in the nineteenth (7:369). Whether one accepts miracles as true or not is not really the issue, Arnold reminds us. The issue is individual righteousness.

Arnold declared on several occasions his satisfaction with *God and the Bible*—once to the editor of the *Contemporary Review* when he was engaged in writing it and again a decade later when he wrote to his American friend, Charles Eliot Norton, about the popular edition about to be printed. To Norton he confessed, "in preparing it for the press I seem to find some chapters in it to be the best prose I have ever succeeded in writing" (*Letters* 2:268). Even so, Robert Super points out that Arnold effected more stylistic revisions in *God and the Bible* from one edition to the next than in any of his other books. His concern about its reception surfaces in the preface which he wrote for the publication of the collected articles in volume form in November 1875. His first sentence signifies his reevaluation of the periodical installments that have appeared in the *Contemporary Review.* He mentions reading back over what he has written and being struck by the need to add to his reproof of German biblical critics "some acknowledgment" of their merits (7:374). He makes explicit his persistent goal of reinforcing previously presented arguments. Nor can he forget the controversy surrounding his work. Several of his comments reveal his concern for clarity. He writes, "In revising the present volume, the suspicion and alarm which its contents, like those of its predecessor, will in some quarters excite, could not but be present to my mind. I hope, however, that I have at last made my aim clear, even to the most suspicious" (7:377). Each of his religous books has pursued an identical end. *God and the Bible,* for example, "clears, develops and defends the positions taken in *Literature and Dogma*" (7:377). Such dedicated attention to the topic has been necessary, for Arnold maintains, "at the present moment two things about the Christian religion must surely be clear to anybody with eyes in his head. One is, that men cannot do without it, the other, that they cannot do with it as it is" (7:378). His intention has ever been to afford the thoughtful individual an "intellectually serious" approach to reading the Bible and receiving Christian teachings without either destroying his faith or compromising his intelligence (7:393).

In 1877 Arnold saw through print *Last Essays on Church and Religion,* a set of four papers he had published separately in journals the preceding year. Two of the articles; "Bishop Butler and the Zeit-Geist" and "A Last Word on the Burials Bill," have a rather tangential connection to his other religious prose. The piece on Butler offers Arnold's tribute to the eighteenth-century English bishop, Joseph Butler, whom Arnold greatly admired and to whom his own religious ideas were heavily indebted. In the other more topical essay, "A Last Word on the Burials Bill," Arnold recommends, to appease Dissenters, several minor changes to the burial office read by Anglican clergymen at services held in parish churchyards.

In a third article entitled "The Church of England," originally presented as a lecture before an audience of clergymen, Arnold endeavors to explain how he can condemn or question much Christian doctrine and still call himself a friend of the Church of England. His support for institutionalized religion derives from his view of the Anglican Church as "a great national society for the promotion of what is commonly called *goodness* . . . through the means of the Christian religion and of the Bible" (8:65). Echoing similar claims made in his earlier religious works about the purpose of the Bible, Arnold argues that promoting goodness is the true "object of the Church" and the true "business of the clergy" (8:66). The foundation of religion and the mission of its ministers are the improvement of conduct, not the promulgation of doctrine. And this may best be effected by a unified national Church.

Time and again in his religious prose Arnold chastises Dissenters—those church-going Philistines. By breaking away from the national church they have promoted cultural dissonance, and in fostering a rigid and repressive theology, they have stifled cultural advancement. The tendency has been regressive rather than progressive. Arnold warns his readers earlier in *St. Paul and Protestantism* to remember that "the Church exists, not for the sake of opinions, but for the sake of moral practice, and a united endeavour after this is stronger than a broken one" (6:97). Because the Anglican Church has resisted very narrow doctrine, it "is more serviceable than Puritanism to religious progress" and thus better suited to be the national Church (6:85). Arnold restates this view (supposedly for the last time) in "The Church of England" (8:86) but amplifies it by noting that, sadly, the viability of the Anglican Church is threatened not just by Dissenting sects but by "the estrangement of the working classes" as well (8:71). Even though clergymen have attempted to improve the living conditions, the "physical well-being," of the working classes, they have not demonstrated "a positive sympathy with popular ideals" (8:76). To many it appears that "the Church shares and serves the prejudices of rank and property, instead of contending with them" (8:74). Such a position not only alienates the masses from the Church but also separates the Church itself from the living ideal of active Christian faith set forth in the Bible. Arnold's essay ends with the reassurance that the Church of England "by placing the stress of its religion on goodness, by cultivating grace and peace . . . will inspire attachment" and will endure (8:86).

The most powerful piece of polemic in the collection and the one most important to a discussion of recursion in Arnold's prose is "A Psychological Parallel," an essay which Ruth apRoberts appropriately labels "a comprehensive reprise" of Arnold's mature religious opinions (259). Arnold has consistently maintained that one may abandon belief in certain aspects of orthodox Christianity—the occurrence of miracles reported in the Bible or the truth of codified Church dogma, for instance—without abandoning Christianity itself. His detractors were not easily convinced, asking if one cannot trust the Church fathers, what remains? Thus, in circular fashion, Arnold returns to where he began, to St. Paul, and confronts the question of whether the teachings of a religious leader such as Paul must be discounted entirely if they cannot be entirely believed. Arnold proposes to answer "by putting a parallel case"—a case that he has already mentioned in passing near the end of *God and the Bible*—that of Sir Matthew Hale (8:113).

Arnold now elects to elaborate on the relevance of his previous allusion to Hale.

Throughout much of the seventeenth century a belief in witchcraft prevailed and "created for the mind an atmosphere from which it was hard to escape" (8:115). Arnold renders a moving account of a witchcraft trial over which the eminent Chief Justice Hale presided—a trial we can now perceive to have been dominated by fear and superstition—that nevertheless resulted in the conviction and execution of the two women accused. Unfortunate as this incident was, it does not indicate that Matthew Hale was unworthy of the high office he held. According to Arnold, "What the trial shows us is, that a man of veracity, judgment, and mental power, may have his mind thoroughly governed, on certain subjects, by a foregone conclusion as to what is likely and credible" (8:121). Hale was as conditioned to believe in demonic possession as St. Paul was to believe in the physical resurrection of Jesus Christ.

Having given an example of a noteworthy countryman with whom his readers are undoubtedly familiar, Arnold advances a second parallel case of a little-known individual who, despite his obscurity, has an even "closer applicability to St. Paul" (8:121). He chooses another seventeenth-century Englishman, the Cambridge Platonist John Smith. An astute, learned churchman, Smith, like Hale, was influenced by the Zeitgeist to accept "the erroneous belief in witchcraft" prevalent in his day (8:127). Even so, Arnold reveals in lengthy excerpts from a sermon Smith preached against witchcraft how he managed to transcend "the common conception" of "diabolical operation" as something "external" to man (8:125). Smith transformed the traditional psychology and arrived at "what was at bottom experimental and real"—the notion that evil dwells *within* human nature (8:126). Smith's contribution thus parallels St. Paul's. Both admit the physical reality of the non-natural, but both add a "truer idea," a spiritual dimension (8:129).

Finally, Arnold considers the possibility that an individual may be unable to believe in the miracles reported in the Bible and yet may belong to the established Church. While the Zeitgeist of the nineteenth century has caused many Victorians to doubt the literal truth of some Church teachings, they may still support the Anglican Church in its principle mission as "a national Christian society for the promotion of goodness" (8:132). In this essay, Arnold repeats his long-standing argument that the Church should relax its emphasis on dogma. He goes so far as to argue that clergymen themselves should not be required to subscribe to the Thirty-nine Articles. He suspects there are many who cannot profess acceptance of all thirty-nine statements who would prove to be dedicated ministers to the true message of Christianity. Arnold is not willing for the Book of Common Prayer to be abandoned though. For the masses of Englishmen, "It has created sentiments deeper than we can see or measure. Our feeling does not connect itself with *any* language about righteousness and religion, but with *that* language" (8:135). The power of the Prayer Book, like the power of the Bible, is literary or poetic and is made manifest by its ability to touch human emotions and inspire right conduct. Arnold advocates using the Prayer Book as one would use the Bible, receiving a portion of the services and creeds as literal truth and reading the rest as the poetic "approximations to a profound truth" (8:136). In Arnold's estimation, "It is a great error to think that whatever is thus perceived to be poetry ceases to be available in religion. The noblest races are those which know how to make the most serious use of poetry" (8:132). In summarizing the thesis of this essay, Arnold is simultaneously summarizing the theses of all his religious prose: "The practical lesson to be drawn from all this is, that we should avoid violent revolution in the words and externals of religion. Profound sentiments are connected with them; they are aimed at the highest good, however imperfectly apprehended. Their form often gives them beauty, the associations which cluster around them give them always pathos and solemnity" (8:142). Arnold thus echoes the claim that he has made from the outset that his intention has been to strengthen the individual's commitment to the Church of England, to encourage his attachment to the Bible, and to motivate his pursuit of right conduct.

From 1870 to 1877 Arnold was preoccupied with religious matters. Essay led to essay, volume to volume as Arnold generated hundreds of pages of dialectic aimed at making "reason and the will of God prevail." Well aware that readers cannot be expected to alter their way of thinking overnight, that attitudes and opinions evolve over time, Arnold worked at making himself understood. At the end of his personal notebook for 1868, he wrote, "He who fancies that his mind may effectually be changed in a short time, deceives himself." [8] In addition, Arnold was extremely sensitive to the reception of his work and consequently willing to devote reams of paper to clarifying his position. If his audience had misread what he wrote or disagreed with it, he would try once again in a new article or lecture to explain himself.

Arnold's prose style and his composition technique were genuinely recursive. He often introduced a new work by quoting himself or closely paraphrasing his own previously expressed views. Individual assertions and entire arguments were effectively impressed upon the audience through frequent repetition. In fact, after reading several of Arnold's works one has difficulty recalling when an idea or catch phrase first surfaced. Ironically, Arnold himself occasionally forgot. In a manuscript letter to Thomas Humphry Ward, undated but probably written in March 1879, Arnold asks, "Do you happen to remember a saying of mine about the superiority of poetic expression over other expression which you quoted in that article of yours in the *Saturday Review*? I have said the same thing very often, but I think what you quoted was my first utterance of it, and I cannot remember where it is. That is the worst of having written so much!" [9] The *best* part of having written so much and having been so widely read is that Arnold can reasonably expect editors and reviewers like Ward to remember his words. Because his prose works build on one another, one of Arnold's contemporaries, John Burroughs, writing for the *Century Magazine* two months after Arnold's death, argues that Matthew Arnold deserves to be read extensively, for only then can he be fully appreciated. In the essays, says Burroughs, "His effect is cumulative; he hits a good many times in the same place, and his work as a whole makes a deeper impression than any single essay of his would seem to warrant." [10] While there is a unity, a coherence to the body of Arnold's prose, there is also meaningful development through expansion and elaboration. Continually striving to practice what he proposes that others do, Matthew Arnold in his religious writings has sought truth—spiritual, literary, and cultural—by approaching it on one side after another.

NOTES

1. Arnold refers to this verbal exchange with his sister in a letter to his mother dated 13 October 1863. George W. E. Russell, ed., *Letters of Matthew Arnold, 1848–1888,* 2 vols. (London: Macmillan, 1895). All other references to the *Letters* are to this edition.

2. To illustrate, when his first prose work, the 1853 preface to his *Poems*, met with hostile reviews, Arnold answered his critics the following year with a "Preface to Second Edition of *Poems*." In this brief notice he explains his decision to allow the first preface to be reprinted with only slight modifications and devotes no more than a few paragraphs to answering his attackers. However, Arnold had not laid the issue to rest. A more elaborate defense appeared three years later in the text of his inaugural lecture as Poetry Chair at Oxford entitled "On the Modern Element in Literature." Other prose pieces were similarly motivated. The ideas Arnold presented in the 1864 Oxford lecture, "The Function of Criticism at the Present Time," were expanded upon his final address at the university in 1867. But that lecture, "Culture and Its Enemies," aroused such scorn that Arnold was prompted to reply—not in one essay but in a series of five. All six were subsequently published together in *Culture and Anarchy* (1869). The same trend can be found in Arnold's later essays on literature and in his works on education and religion. See Sidney Coulling, *Matthew Arnold and His Critics: A Study of Arnold's Controversies* (Athens: Ohio University Press, 1974), and R. H. Super, ed., *The Complete Prose Works of Matthew Arnold,* 11 vols. (Ann Arbor: University of Michigan Press, 1960–77, hereafter *CPW*).

3. For discussions of Arnold's moral and religious ideas, see Ruth ap-Roberts, *Arnold and God* (Berkeley and Los Angeles: University of California Press, 1983); A. O. J. Cockshut, *The Unbelievers: English Agnostic Thought, 1840–1890* (New York: New York University Press, 1966); Dorothea Krook, *Three Traditions of Moral Thought* (Cambridge: Cambridge University Press, 1959); James C. Livingston, *Matthew Arnold and Christianity* (Columbia: University of South Carolina Press, 1986); and William Robbins, *The Ethical Idealism of Matthew Arnold: A Study of the Nature and Sources of His Moral and Religious Ideas* (Toronto: University of Toronto Press, 1959). For analysis of Arnold's rhetoric, see John Holloway, *The Victorian Sage* (London: Macmillan, 1953), pp. 202–43.

4. While addition or expansion was Arnold's more typical method of revi-

sion, he did some years after their original release prepare cheaper, abridged "popular" editions of three of his religious books. The popular edition of *Literature and Dogma*, published in London by Smith, Elder and in New York by Macmillan, was the first of the three to appear in 1883; Smith, Elder issued the popular edition of *God and the Bible* in 1884 and the popular edition of *St. Paul and Protestantism* in 1887. Significantly, Arnold did not publish these eclipsed versions until the full-length editions had run through multiple printings.

5. Ruth apRoberts, "The Classics Canon of Matthew Arnold" (Paper presented at the Modern Language Association Convention in New York on 29 December 1986).

6. Arnold's propensity for coining terms and phrases is well-known and is another example of his tendency to popularize his ideas by quoting himself. From his advocacy of "sweetness and light," the "disinterestedness" of the critical spirit, and learning "the best that is known and thought in the world" to his recommendation of applying "touchstones of taste" in the evaluation of literature and the "method of culture" to the struggle against Philistine complacency, Arnold capsulized his theories in memorable phrases which echo throughout the body of his prose. David Riede argues persuasively, however, that Arnold is ironically "betrayed" by the very medium he relies upon. Arnold settles for repeating terms and phrases rather than defining them. His language is self-referential in that "it refers only to other words, not to things." Or as scholars such as J. Hillis Miller and W. David Shaw would have it, Arnold's famous phrases are "empty linguistic shells" or "empty signifiers." Arnold defended his use of catchy phrases in a letter of 5 April 1869 to his mother, saying "The merit of terms of this sort is that they fix in people's minds the *things* to which they refer" (quoted in *CPW* 5:415). See Riede, *Matthew Arnold and the Betrayal of Language* (Charlottesville: University Press of Virginia, 1988); Miller, *The Disappearance of God* (Cambridge: Harvard University Press, 1963); and Shaw, "The Agnostic Imagination in Victorian Poetry," *Criticism* 22 (Spring 1980): 125–31.

7. In fact, Arnold attempted to render this service to education in a more direct way in 1872 by editing for young readers chapters forty through sixty-six of Isaiah. Entitled *A Bible Reading for Schools*, it was widely adopted as a textbook. *Isaiah of Jerusalem*, a companion edition of the first thirty-nine chapters, appeared in 1883. Arnold believed study of the Bible an ideal way to bring children into "contact with poetry and philosophy," thereby advancing the aims of culture (7:412).

8. Notebook entry for 29 December 1868, Beinecke Library, Yale University.

9. Manuscript letter to Thomas Humphry Ward, Cobham, n.d. [? March 1879], Beinecke Library, Yale University.

10. John Burroughs, "Matthew Arnold's Criticism," *Century Magazine* 36 (June 1888): 185–94. Quoted in Carl Dawson and John Pfordresher, *Matthew Arnold: The Critical Heritage* (London: Routledge and Kegan Paul, 1979), p. 392.

9

Hardy's Retroactive Self-Censorship: The Case of *The Well-Beloved*

Anne C. Pilgrim

From his earliest days as a novelist, Thomas Hardy presented his works to the public in two successive ways, first in serial installments in a periodical, and then in volume form. Beginning with his composition of *Far from the Madding Crowd* in 1874, he ran into the nervousness of editors who requested discreet alterations to his periodical stories; it was Leslie Stephen of the *Cornhill* who wanted him to "omit the baby" from the scene in which Bathsheba Everdene opens Fanny Robin's coffin, and who also suggested that "if the omission were made it might be restored on republication."[1] By the closing stages of his novel-writing career in the 1890s, Hardy had become inured to the necessity of bowdlerizing the manuscripts of his novels for their first appearance and then restoring the materials which had been perceived as likely to give offense when the novels appeared in volume form. It is well known to students of Hardy that the versions of *Tess of the d'Urbervilles* which appeared in the *Graphic* and of *Jude the Obscure* which appeared in *Harper's New Monthly Magazine* were heavily censored by Hardy. What is much less well known is that on one occasion, in producing his last published novel *The Well-Beloved,* Hardy worked in the opposite manner. In this instance, the serial text, dating from 1892, represented his original intention, and he substantially revised it later in such a way as to remove elements that might create difficulties when the novel came out in book form in 1897. The reasons for and the nature of this revision form the subject of this paper.

Although according to Hardy the story had been "sketched many years before"[2] its serial publication, he did not write it until late in 1891, as a consequence then of having promised "something light"[3] and considerably briefer to Tillotson and Son to replace the serial version of *Tess of the d'Urbervilles,* then known as *Too Late Beloved,* which Tillotson's had found entirely unsuitable for publication some two years before. The replacement tale, under the title *The Pursuit of the Well-Beloved,* and a subtitle, "A Sketch of a Temperament," ran weekly from 1 October to 17 December 1892 in the *Illustrated London News.* Not only was the story "light," it was more than a little fantastic, a study of the artistic temperament rather than a dully realistic history, as the following necessarily condensed account of it will show.

The original plot, in thirty-three chapters, traces the romantic adventures of Jocelyn Pearston, a gifted young sculptor of twenty who returns from London to visit his Wessex home on the Isle of Slingers (i.e., Portland Bill). A lover of beauty for whom the abstract idea of the Well-Beloved has already been embodied in many successive female forms, he now concludes that the Well-Beloved has decided to remain in Avice Caro, a young island neighbour to whom he becomes engaged. But the Well-Beloved abruptly migrates into the person of Marcia Bencomb, whom he takes back to London and impulsively marries. Quarrels, regrets and recriminations ensue; among the few things the pair agrees on are the defects of matrimony, their need for a permanent separation (Marcia departs to the Pacific coast of America), and their freedom to form new ties. The story moves forward to find Jocelyn at the age of forty returning to the island for the funeral of Avice Caro and discovering his Well-

Beloved in her daughter Ann Avice; his intention to marry her is checked only by his learning that she is secretly married already. In Part Third, after another twenty-year interval, he visits the now widowed Ann Avice, and meets her elegant, rather too-docile daughter Avice; this time he succeeds in marrying this final incarnation of the Well-Beloved despite the great difference in their ages. His second marriage is also a disaster, for two reasons: Avice's physical aversion to Pearston and the surprise return of her true love Henri Leverre. She finds her husband truly magnanimous: he does not assert his right to sexual relations and in fact hatches a plan to leave the two young people free to marry. He places advertisements for his long lost wife so that he will be able to pretend to find her and leave Avice free. The serial has an ironic and painful surprise ending: Marcia does in fact answer his appeal, and the still-youthful Pearston finds that his lifelong pursuit of beauty is to end in his being yoked with a hideously aged wife who has returned for good.

There is no evidence that in 1892 Hardy regarded his story as suitable for publication in book form; in fact there is some firm evidence of his doubts in that regard. Early in 1892, when Harper and Brothers had already secured the rights to the American serial publication, they conveyed through their London agents Osgood and McIlvaine their readiness both to publish it in book form and to allow Hardy the opportunity to revise it. Hardy's reply displayed his usual canny prudence in managing his literary affairs: while agreeing that Harper and Brothers might publish the American edition of the volume form, and even discussing possible terms, he stipulated that "the story being short and slight and written entirely with a view to serial publication, it may be found upon consideration to be inadvisable in the interest of future novels to issue this as a book at all; hence I reserve the right to withhold it in that form either altogether, or until the story can be re-written."[4]

In fact four years went by before he picked the story up again, an extremely busy and eventful period in his career. As well as writing verse destined to appear in *Wessex Poems,* writing short stories, and collecting his others into the 1893 volume *Life's Little*

Ironies, Hardy wrote and published *Jude the Obscure,* a major novel into which he poured his energies; he was involved in on-the-scene research and in a year and a half of writing, as well as in the extra task of bowdlerizing the novel for its serial publication and restoring it in the summer of 1895 for its appearance in book form in November of that year. Overlapping with the final stages of work on *Jude,* starting early in 1895, was Hardy's contribution in the form of textual work (revision, corrections, and the writing of new prefaces) to the first uniform edition of his Wessex novels, in sixteen volumes, being brought out by Osgood, McIlvaine. The first edition of *Jude* appeared as Volume VIII in the series, and as publication rights to such very early novels as *Desperate Remedies* lapsed, Osgood, McIlvaine added them to the collected edition. The sixteenth and last volume was *Under the Greenwood Tree,* in September 1896. Much of this latter textual work by Hardy was carried on under the strain of the sometimes violently adverse reaction to the frankness of *Jude,* and it is little wonder that after writing his preface to *Under the Greenwood Tree* in August he embarked on an eight-week holiday with his wife.

Hardy, now in his late fifties, was avowedly anxious—had been so for some years—to return to his primary vocation as a poet after more than a quarter century devoted to fiction. He did not do so immediately, however, for in the last months of 1896 he agreed—whether at his own suggestion or that of his publishers is not known—to revise *The Pursuit of the Well-Beloved* for publication as a belated seventeenth volume in the uniform edition. His motives for doing so may have been gratified vanity, in finding that Osgood, McIlvaine considered it worthy of inclusion, or a prudent concern with keeping his name before the public in the interval before his first book of poems could appear. Certainly to some extent they must have been financial, for Osgood, McIlvaine was generous with royalties (in the case of their six-shilling edition of *Jude* they returned one shilling six pence of the price of each copy sold to the author),[5] and the 1891 passage of the American Copyright Act had meant that for each novel from *Tess* onward Hardy could count on receiving royalties from any and all American publishers of his work. As his biographer

Michael Millgate points out, Hardy was looking forward to becoming "a retired novelist living on the proceeds of past work;"[6] these proceeds could be—and in fact were—significantly enhanced by royalties from *The Well-Beloved.*

Although Hardy's doubts as expressed in 1892 about the advisability of issuing his story as a book were overcome, he stood by his right to revise it, not just because of his dissatisfaction with a work that had been "written entirely with a view to serial publication" but also because of developments in the meantime. The revised version which appeared on 16 March 1897 suggests by the nature of the revisions—particularly the excision from the plot of Jocelyn's two unfortunate marriages—Hardy's response to three things: the 1895 publication of *Jude the Obscure,* the December 1896 publication of Richard Le Gallienne's novel *The Quest of the Golden Girl,* and Hardy's new and recent wish on the eve of his return to poetry to be conciliatory toward those whom he had lately offended—both his wife Emma and his reading public—by his tendentious attacks on marriage and his aggressive frankness about the role of sexuality in human relations.

Certain elements in each of the two novels which had appeared in the four years since his serial left Hardy open to the same imputation, that of a lack of originality: readers of a merely reprinted *Pursuit of the Well-Beloved* might infer that he owed a debt either to his own novel or to Le Gallienne's. To modern scholars it is clear that *The Pursuit of the Well-Beloved* was a preliminary treatment of issues which Hardy was to expand upon in *Jude*; however, to most of the readers of his novels, the serial was unknown (one observer said of it that "it seems . . . to have made little impression at the time"),[7] and a reader who had just recently finished *Jude,* or had even merely heard about it, might well conclude that Hardy was repeating himself if the serial version were not reworked. In his first marriage Jocelyn is all too like Jude: he contracts an early marriage unwisely and suffers for it; he finds himself involved with a strong-willed woman who is very articulate in her denunciation of marriage as an institution and who has "advanced views."[8] Marcia recalls both Arabella Donn, in her sensual appeal and her willingness to depart to the far side of the world, and Sue Bridehead. In his second marriage Pearston even more closely resembles Sue's husband Richard Phillotson, who declines to force himself on a fastidious young wife and sends her back to the arms of her youthful lover; in his letters he confides in his friend Alfred Somers as Phillotson does in his friend George Gillingham. As for the other novel, it seems merely an accident of literary history that Le Gallienne's *Quest of the Golden Girl* should come on the scene just as Hardy was about to reissue his *Pursuit of the Well-Beloved.* Again, Hardy risked the imputation of debt where none was owed. Le Gallienne, an active journalist and reviewer, had of course had the opportunity to read Hardy's serial story, although his whimsical tale told by a poet of thirty who goes on a walking tour in search of the perfect woman—his Golden Girl—to make his wife owes much more to Sterne's *A Sentimental Journey* in the looseness of its structure and even in specific episodes, as well as in its sexual suggestiveness (its narrator is a lingerie fetichist and a libertine). Its ending managed to be both improper and mawkish, as the quester recognizes his true love in a Picadilly prostitute and marries her, only to have her die giving birth to a daughter and instructing him to "let her be your little golden girl."[9] The romance was an immediate success; a thousand copies were sold on publication day. One can only imagine Hardy's dismay at the thought that his novel might, especially if it retained its original title, invite comparison of the two.

After the fact, Hardy maintained that he had not been able to revise his serial as completely as he had intended,[10] but he did make many changes, both aesthetically and prudentially dictated, which went far beyond the shortening of his title to *The Well-Beloved.* He made a number of incidental improvements such as changing the spelling of his hero's name to Pierston, thereby clarifying the pronunciation and adding an appropriate marine allusion. He added poetic epigraphs, from Crashaw, Wyatt, and Shakespeare, to each part; tinkered with chapter titles; and made Pierston "A Young Man of 60" rather than of 59 at the outset of Part Third to enhance the symmetry of the tale. In other larger ways Hardy increased the geometric precision of the three-generation plot. He lopped off altogether an initial brief episode of Pierston in London burning love letters from smitten girls (eight names are specified) and thus started the action with Pierston's arrival on the island—a "return of the native" motif which reviewers were quick to spot—and his discovery of Avice Caro, the first of the three Avices, *none* of whom he will, in the new version, marry. Major changes include having Pierston stop short of marrying Marcia in Part First, and a completely rewritten ending, in which the last seven chapters of the serial were removed and four new ones substituted. The effects of these latter changes must now be considered.

By having Pierston and Marcia quarrel and part before marrying, Hardy was able to excise from his novel passages that sound very much like ones in *Jude*—the sort of remarks about marriage that had made Mrs. Oliphant in January 1896 describe that novel as "intended as an assault on the stronghold of marriage, which is now beleaguered on every side." [11] Barely is the couple home from the honeymoon, in the serial, before their regrets make them talk "in complete accord of the curse of matrimony." "In their ill-matched junction on the strength of a two or three days' passion," the narrator observes, "they felt the full irksomeness of a formal tie," [12] an insight identical to Jude's into his marriage with Arabella: "Their lives were ruined, he thought; ruined by the fundamental error of their matrimonial union: that of having based a permanent contract on a temporary feeling which had no necessary connection with affinities that alone render a life-long comradeship tolerable." [13] Not only their foolish haste but the nature of marriage itself is assailed by Marcia, who divines that she is "her husband's property, like one of his statues that he could not sell." [14] Marcia, like Sue, has reason to view the marriage tie with suspicion, and since the story is set back in the 1850s she has not even the possibility of divorce to rely on. Her "advanced views" at the point of marital separation include an assertion that "I fail to see why, in making each our own home, we should not make our own matrimonial laws if we choose." [15] Following up on this radical notion, both she and Pearston contract bigamous second marriages, a fact which Hardy skims over lightly in the serial but which he was no doubt happy enough to eradicate from his more conventional book version.

In his reworking of the novel's ending, Hardy once again prevented a marriage founded on doubtful motives from taking place. Pierston wishes to marry the third Avice at least partly as a way of making amends for having abandoned the first, and she agrees to their engagement out of a wish to please and comfort her dying mother. The more timely reappearance of Henri Leverre, in the new version, and Avice's elopement with him on the eve of her wedding to Pierston places a counteremphasis on mutuality and youthful passion and introduces as well the idea of poetic justice. Pierston refuses to blame his vanished bride, saying "She didn't make the circumstances. I did. . . . It was how I served her grandmother." [16] Pierston's generosity to Avice remains, but in the later version he is no longer called upon to be the generous-though-rebuffed elderly husband. By deleting their marriage, Hardy was able to omit from his text material that was troublesome both because it was indelicate in nature and because it so closely resembled that in *Jude*. The serial had dwelt, even in its chapter titles, on the idea of possession. Two of these titles which disappeared in revision were those for Chapter XXVII, "He desperately clutches the form [of the Well-Beloved]," and for Chapter XXVIII, in which is described the early married life of Pearston and Avice, "He possesses it; he possesses it not." Whether the idea is one of sequence or of simultaneity, it draws the reader's attention to the question of a husband's rights. Like Sue Bridehead, Avice in the serial displays nervousness, apprehension, and repugnance; when Pearston, listening at the door of her room, accidentally brushes against the handle, he hears her "gasp and start." [17] Like Phillotson, Pearston is noble, compassionate, and free-thinking; he repudiates legalities he sees as unjust, declaring that "to me healthy natural instinct is true law, and not an Act of Parliament." [18] Sincere such declarations no doubt were, on the part of both character and author, but by 1896 they must have come to seem needlessly provocative.

Pierston in the later version is much more of an artist—a lover of beauty in the abstract—and a dreamer than he is an amorist, for in the general reduction of the attention given to sexual matters in *The Well-Beloved* Hardy drastically reduced his hero's sexual experience. The Pierston of the 1897 book version is not in his early youth so successful a lover that he has a large bundle of letters to dispose of; he does not marry a Junoesque island girl and live with her for four years; he does not marry and possess, however briefly, an eighteen-year-old when he is sixty; in fact he does not marry at all until Marcia returns to his side and he offers her "such friendship as I am capable of. . . till the end."[19] His bride, when he finally has one, is so advanced in age and decrepitude (and presumably sexlessness) that she suffers an attack of rheumatism on their wedding day and "after being well wrapped up" is "wheeled into the church in a chair."[20] Were it not for Pierston's few days of cohabitation with Marcia long before, one might believe him altogether virginal.

In both accounts Marcia, after her departure from London, has been married and widowed and on her return is discovered to be, rather improbably, stepmother to the youngest Avice's true love, Henri Leverre. The treatment of her return in each case is drastically different, however, and indicates a major shift in attitude on Hardy's part. In the serial her reappearance when least wanted seems the expression of a cosmic joke at Pearston's expense, and the closing chapter ends with his bitter laughter, "so violent as to be an agony."[21] In the new version Marcia returns out of concern for her stepson and transfers that concern to Pierston, especially when he falls ill; in the final chapter she shares with him in the experience of loss, renunciation, and resignation which gives the ending its muted tone. After his illness Pierston discovers that he has lost his artistic sense, his care for beauty, and in relief exclaims, "Thank Heaven I am old at last."[22] He leaves London forever, accompanied by Marcia who has also accepted her true age by presenting her face to Pierston's eyes denuded of all the "beautifying artifices"[23] she is skilled in applying after a lifetime in society. Thus reduced, they return to the island for the last time and marry for convenience and companionship.

Virtually from the day of publication it was apparent that Hardy's scheme of purifying *The Pursuit of the Well-Beloved* had been successful. Only four days later, on 20 March, the *Graphic* proclaimed in an editorial that Mrs. Grundy would be happy with Hardy, since there was nothing in *The Well-Beloved* to bring a blush "to even the most inflammable cheek of maidenhood";[24] on the same day, an unsigned article in the *Saturday Review* welcomed Hardy back "to his own province of the imagination," contrasting *The Well-Beloved*'s "preoccupation with beauty" to the ugliness of *Tess* and *Jude*, which had been "of set purpose squalid."[25] As the weeks elapsed in the spring of 1897, reviewers on both sides of the Atlantic echoed this initial expression of pleasure and relief. The *Literary World* noted that *The Well-Beloved* had "few features in common with its two most recent predecessors" and was "free from the grosser traits that sent staid matrons into hysterics of wrath";[26] the *Athenaeum* dourly referred to it as "a more pleasing sample of Mr. Hardy's later manner than some we could name" and expressed the hope that its appearance indicated "a desire to renew those pleasant relations with his readers that should never have been interrupted."[27] American journals also contrasted the new work to *Jude* in particular. William Lyon Phelps, writing in the *Book Buyer* in May, launched into a food metaphor, acclaiming *The Well-Beloved* as a dish more "palatable" which would "take out the taste of *Jude the Obscure*." The new work is "innocuous" and makes him exclaim, "For this relief much thanks."[28] Not all critics were aware that the novel had appeared some years before as a serial, and those who mentioned the serial of 1892 were not always aware that it had been revised. One of these was William Morton Payne, who confessed in the *Dial* of Chicago his wish "that *The Well-Beloved* were a recently-written book, for it would represent a reaction from the mood of cynical bitterness that has been upon Mr. Hardy of late, and all lovers of good literature would rejoice to learn that the 'blue devils' had been exorcised, and to find the novelist of *Far from the Madding Crowd* and *A Pair of Blue Eyes* restored to them. Such 'a return of the native' to his old-time scenes and themes would be welcome indeed."[29]

The intensity of Hardy's desire to succeed in disarming the reviewers at this delicate moment in his career may perhaps be gauged by his overreaction to one extremely negative anonymous review, "Thomas Hardy, Humorist," in the London *World*. It appeared barely a week after the release of *The Well-Beloved*, on 24 March, and Hardy could certainly not foresee that it would be the only such attack on his work among more than two dozen reviews to come; still, he reacted with outrage and even a degree of panic, sending a flurry of letters from his Dorchester home to friends and literary associates. In two letters written on the same day, to Edmund Gosse and to Florence Henniker, he complained of the "extraordinary stab in the back"[30] and the "horrid stab"[31] delivered to his "poor little innocent book,"[32] and expressed his amazement that it could give any offense. To Gosse he explained that "one of the reasons why I consented to the reprinting of such a bygone, wildly romantic fancy was that it wd please Mrs. Grundy & her young Person, & her respected husband, by its absolutely 'harmless' quality"; to Mrs. Henniker he said that "one of my reasons for letting the story be reprinted was that it cd not by any possibility offend Mr. or Mrs. Grundy, or their Young Persons." The references to consenting and reprinting seem more than a little disingenuous; it is hard to believe that Hardy had forgotten his own activity and the extensive revisions he had so recently made.

Hardy's agitation is understandable, however, for the review in the *World*, which was both malicious and mendacious, posed a distinct threat to his plan to foster the public perception of *The Well-Beloved* as "harmless." From the start, the unknown reviewer adopted a tone of sneering sarcasm, calling the new novel an example of "the later Hardy at his best—so tasteful, reticent and amiable"[33] while singling out for attention any hint of the fleshly which could, with difficulty, be found in it. He (or she—there was some speculation later that a woman had written it) objected to a passage describing Pierston's progress through a crowded reception room with a close-up view of "shoulder-blades, back hair, glittering headgear, necknapes, moles, hairpins, pearl-powder, pimples," et cetera; remarked on his being diverted from Avice Caro "by the more opulent attractions" of Marcia; found a deliberate reference to the flesh in the choice of surname for Avice ("*Caro, carnis* is the noun with the declension of which Mr. Hardy is perpetually and everlastingly preoccupied in his new book"); and ended a long paragraph with a punning condemnation: "Of all forms of sex-mania in fiction we have no hesitation in pronouncing the most unpleasant to be the Wessex-mania of Mr. Thomas Hardy." Two sentences, coming at the end of a flippant passage of plot summary, must have been particularly enraging. In them the reader was told "Avice III elopes with the stepson of Marcia, and Marcia, now a faded and painted harridan, returns to appropriate the senile amorist. And thus ends Mr. Thomas Le Gallienne Hardy's *Pursuit of the Golden Girl.*" Le Gallienne's hero had found his wife among the "poor painted faces"[34] clustering at street corners in Picadilly; the use of the adjective here unfairly blackened the character of Marcia, while the blending of the authors' names and the two titles impugned Hardy's originality.

His worst fears were thus realized; his revisions had gone for naught, or so it seemed for the moment. In fact Hardy received prompt reassurances and support of several kinds, including an invitation, which he declined, to reply directly to the *World* in the pages of the *Academy.* His friend Gosse, who had written the *Saturday Review* article, sprang into action and wrote another favorable review, this time signed, for the *St. James's Gazette* of 31 March. Unexpected assistance came from Le Gallienne himself, whom Hardy knew only slightly; the younger man quickly produced a piece for the *London Star* of 29 March in which he deplored the outcry "which already mounts to heaven from Philistia"[35] and observed that Hardy's novel invited comparison with *Liber Amoris* but was clearly superior to Hazlitt's work. He thus attempted to throw readers off the scent of his *Golden Girl* and—not incidentally—to promote his own 1893 edition of *Liber Amoris,* the only one then available. In the long run, Hardy had in fact nothing to worry about; favorable reviews continued to appear, and the sales of *The Well-Beloved* were excellent (it was mentioned in the April *Bookman* as one of the month's bestsellers).[36] Still, he was not easily or soon mollified. When sorting the materials, over twenty years later, for the second part of his autobiography, *The Later Years of Thomas Hardy,* he saved and had reprinted in Chapter 4 extracts from three separate letters of his, defending *The Well-Beloved* against this one "ferocious review."[37]

Other students of Hardy's work and his publishing career have commented, in various ways, on Hardy's revision of his serial into the novel *The Well-Beloved*. Both versions of the story, but especially the later one, have been scrutinized for covert autobiography, whether crudely by Lois Deacon and Terry Coleman in their 1966 "exposé" of Hardy's relations with his cousin Tryphena Sparks, or more subtly and plausibly by others, such as Michael Millgate. Macmillan's New Wessex edition of the novel, published in 1975, includes an introduction by J. Hillis Miller, in which he provides a psychoanalytic reading of the plot and finds that "a reading of the two versions reinforces the reader's sense that the novel is contrived, fantastic, openly fictional"; he sees in Hardy's "late Victorian novel a text which anticipates twentieth-century experimentation,"[38] such as that carried on by John Fowles and J. L. Borges. A more precise parallel to Hardy's substitution of one ending for another, however, is one which Miller mentions only in passing, that is, Dickens's reworking of the ending of *Great Expectations* in 1861 at the instance of his friend Bulwer-Lytton, who argued successfully to have the first ending withdrawn and replaced by one which, Dickens agreed, would make "the story . . . more acceptable through the alteration."[39] My account of the revision process with respect to *The Well-Beloved* has emphasized for the first time similar motives of prudence and expediency, revealing the amount of energy, skill, and determination Hardy put into manipulating for his own ends the conditions of Victorian novel publication, and his success in doing so. One of the pleasant ironies of this often ironical history lies in the reassurance held out to Victorian readers by Gosse in his first review of *The Well-Beloved*: "Mr. Hardy," he said, "is an artist of pure race, and no living writer is less moved by the laws of supply and demand. We must take what he chooses to give us; it is quite certain that he never allows himself to ask what we should like to receive."[40]

NOTES

1. Leslie Stephen, letter to Hardy, 13 April 1874, in *Thomas Hardy: A Bibliographical Study*, by Richard Little Purdy (London: Oxford University Press, 1954), app. II, p. 339.

2. Florence Emily Hardy, *The Later Years of Thomas Hardy* (London: Macmillan, 1930), p. 59.

3. Purdy, p. 94.

4. Harper and Brothers Contract Book VI, Columbia University Libraries, pp. 453–54.

5. Letter to Clarence McIlvaine, 24 February 1895, in *The Collected Letters of Thomas Hardy*, ed. Richard Little Purdy and Michael Millgate (Oxford: Clarendon Press, 1980), 2:69 (hereafter *Collected Letters*).

6. Michael Millgate, *Thomas Hardy: A Biography* (Oxford: Oxford University Press, 1982), p. 323.

7. William Morton Payne, "Recent Fiction," *Dial* (Chicago), 16 May 1897, p. 307.

8. Thomas Hardy, *The Pursuit of the Well-Beloved*, *Illustrated London News*, 15 October 1892, p. 481 (hereafter abbreviated *ILN*).

9. Richard Le Gallienne, *The Quest of the Golden Girl* (London and New York: John Lane, 1896), p. 307.

10. *Collected Letters*, 2:152.

11. M. O. W. Oliphant, "The Anti-Marriage League," *Blackwood's Magazine*, January 1896, p. 141.

12. *ILN*, 15 October 1892, p. 481.

13. Thomas Hardy, *Jude the Obscure* (London: Macmillan, 1974), p. 90.

14. *ILN*, 15 October 1892, p. 481.

15. Ibid.

16. Thomas Hardy, *The Well-Beloved* (London: Macmillan, 1975), p. 176.

17. *ILN*, 10 December 1892, p. 743.

18. *ILN*, 17 December 1892, p. 774.

19. Hardy, *The Well-Beloved*, p. 192.

20. Ibid.

21. *ILN*, 17 December 1892, p. 775.

22. Hardy, *The Well-Beloved*, p. 190.

23. Ibid., p. 188.

24. *Graphic*, 20 March 1897, p. 354.

25. *Saturday Review*, 20 March 1897, p. 296.

26. *Literary World*, 26 March 1897, p. 283.

27. *Athenaeum*, 10 April 1897, p. 471.

28. "Incomparable Wessex, Again," *Book Buyer* (New York), May 1897, p. 410.

29. *Dial*, 16 May 1897, p. 307.

30. Hardy to Edmund Gosse, 31 March 1897, *Collected Letters*, 2:156.

31. Hardy to Florence Henniker, 31 March 1897, *Collected Letters*, 2:157.

32. This phrase was directed to Mrs. Henniker, 31 March 1897, *Collected Letters,* 2:157; to Gosse he described *The Well-Beloved* as his "poor innocent little tale," 31 March 1897, *Collected Letters,* 2:156.

33. *World,* 24 March 1897, p. 13. All passages quoted appear on this page.

34. Le Gallienne, p. 294.

35. *Star,* 29 March 1897, p. 1.

36. *Bookman,* April 1897, p. 4.

37. Florence Emily Hardy, p. 61.

38. J. Hillis Miller, introduction to *The Well-Beloved,* p. 17.

39. Dickens's letter to John Forster, 26 June 1861, quoted in *Charles Dickens: His Tragedy and Triumph,* by Edgar Johnson (New York: Simon and Schuster, 1952), 2:969.

40. *Saturday Review,* 20 March 1897, p. 297.

10

Entombing the Angel: Patmore's Revisions of *Angel in the House**

Linda K. Hughes

The case of Coventry Patmore could be a prime instance in the recent tendency to question whether the author's final text is the most desirable one. As Jerome McGann remarks, "Establishing texts for editions too often begins and ends in the pursuit of the so-called author's intentions or author's final intentions (as if these were definitive matters, or as if the author could or even should exercise an exclusive authority over the use of his works)."[1] Patmore's revisions of *Angel in the House* have, understandably, received most attention for the role Gerard Manley Hopkins had in them,[2] though attention has also been directed to his changes in rhythm and meter[3] and to his simplification of the poem's format.[4] It seems far more profitable to see what Patmore lost, however, rather than what he gained, in changing the first edition of *Angel in the House*. What increasingly disappears between the first and the last edition is a sense of women

*This essay was written with the support of a National Endowment for the Humanities Interpretive Research grant.

as living presences. Though of course women are allowed to exist only within narrowly prescribed limits even in the first edition, they become in the standard author's edition far more disembodied and reified, far more relegated to the status of symbols manipulated for artistic purposes. Far more in the final than in the first edition, that is, the female becomes entombed, drained of life and vitality and encased in form. This phenomenon is related to the literal entombment of Patmore's first wife Emily after the first edition appeared but also suggests larger issues involving publication format and the dynamics of revision itself.

The 1949 Oxford volume of Patmore's poems, edited by Frederick Page, is now standard and is based on Patmore's final revision completed in 1886.[5] The first edition differs startlingly from the standard edition in format, since the poem originally appeared in parts and in two different media over a nine-year time span. The first two parts, *The Betrothal* and *The Espousals,* were published anonymously in 1854 and 1856. The third part, *Faithful for Ever,* appeared in 1860, and *The Victories of Love* was first published in three monthly parts in *Macmillan's Magazine* from October through December in 1861. The fourth part was then issued in volume form in 1863. In the standard edition the corresponding materials are presented as two separate poems, *The Angel in the House,* comprising two books ("The Betrothal" and "The Espousals"), and *The Victories of Love,* also comprising two books ("Faithful for Ever" and "Victories of Love," the latter dated, surprisingly, 1862).

This formatting change is understandable. The tone and substance of the 1860, 1861, and 1863 works, as well as the presentation of the female heroine, differed markedly from those of the volumes issued in the 1850s, and *Faithful for Ever* and *Victories of Love* were decidedly less popular than the earlier, more idealized, parts. Yet Patmore's endnote to the 1863 volume clearly indicates that he thought of all four parts as elements of a single poem: "The plan of the Poem, or series of Poems, of which this volume is the conclusion, involved, as it was schemed more than fourteen years ago, a final section on the subject of the hope which remains for individual love in death." The endnote also indicates an important factor in the poem's cessation, a factor that was also to bear on the revisions he carried out:

> It is well, perhaps, for the interests of poetry in this great and hitherto unapproached theme, that my weak voice has been hushed. I no longer have, at every step, the needful encouragement of an approval which was all that my heart valued of fame; I can no longer feel that lively pleasure in the perfection of verbal expression for its own sake, without which such perfection cannot be obtained; nor have I the aid of a criticism to which, I am bound to confess,—now the critic does not forbid the confession,—that every page is more or less indebted for such truth and grace as it may have.

Viewing the four separate volumes as part of one poem is important not only because characters from the first two installments reappear in the last two but also because seeing the two principal female characters of the series in fundamental relation to each other modifies our perception of the female image as a whole.

The difference between the first and standard editions' approaches to women is evident in the prologue to *The Betrothal,* the first volume in the series. In both, the poet and his wife discuss, on their anniversary, the poem he is to write. On the next anniversary the husband produces the first book, which relates the courtship and betrothal of Honoria Churchill and Felix Vaughan, characters explicitly based on the husband and wife of the prologue. But after the initial discussion of the poet's theme and the poem's future in the standard edition, the wife's mind and presence are effaced as the husband assumes the mantle of his poetic vocation:

> She laugh'd. How proud she always was
> To feel how proud he was of her!
> But he had grown distraught, because
> The muse's mood began to stir.
>
> His purpose with performance crown'd,
> He to his well-pleased Wife rehears'd,

When next their Wedding-Day came round,
His leisure's labour, 'Book the First.'
(1886:63)[6]

In the first edition of 1854, in contrast, the husband and wife are collaborators, she the critic rather than passive recipient of his verses:

She laugh'd. How proud she always was
To see how proud he was of her!
Then, arguing high artistic laws,
Long did they o'er the plan confer.
'Twas fix'd, with much on both sides said,
The Song should have no incidents,
They are so dull, and pall, twice read:
Its scope should be the heart's events:
Their Salisbury, for the verse unfit,
They settled last should Sarum be;
And, not to wake their neighbour's wit,
He Felix, and Honoria she.

His purpose with performance crown'd,
To her, kind critic, he rehears'd,
When next their Wedding-Day came round,
His leisure's labour, "Book the First."
(1854:7)

This contrast between a passive, disembodied female auditor and an active mind and presence extends to other elements in the poem. Generally the preludes to each narrative idyl, called "Accompaniments" in the first edition, do not vary substantively in ideology or sentiment from the 1854 to the 1886 versions of the poem, though Patmore considerably rearranged the placement of these lyrics over the years. These lyrics promote an image of woman as object of desire and agency of male aspiration and articulate Patmore's theology. The accompaniment preceding Idyl 5 in the 1854 *Betrothal,* however, has no counterpart in the final edition. In both versions the fifth narrative section is preceded by an opening lyric (called "The Parallel" in 1854, "The Comparison" in 1886) which pits women's inherent innocence against men's propensity to sin and error.[7] In 1886 this is followed by a lyric entitled "Love in Tears" (which, in the first edition, served as an accompaniment for Idyl 8). In 1854 "The Parallel" continued in a second section completely missing from the 1886 volume:

> Her privilege, not impotence,
>   Exempts her from the work of man:
> Humbling his proper excellence,
>   Jeanne d'Arc led war's obstreperous van:
> No post of policy or pride
>   Does Heaven from her holding grudge:
> Miriam and Anna prophesied,
>   In Israel Deborah was judge;
> Countless the Christian heroines
>   Who've blest the world, and still do bless;
> The praise their equal courage wins
>   Counts tenfold through their tenderness;
> And, ah, sad times gone by, denied
>   The joyfullest omen ever seen,
> The full-grown Lion's power and pride
>   Led by the soft hands of a Queen.
>
> (1854:72–73)

This passage is followed by a third section of "The Parallel," which reverts to conventional gender roles for women (women and men are "Well-match'd in all that love requires, / If she's incomparably fair, / And he incomparably admires" [1854:73]). Yet despite its predictable culmination the preliminary matter of Idyl 5 acknowledged a tradition of active and capable women which was then effaced in the final edition.

The concluding sections of the 1854 versus 1886 *Betrothal* also differ significantly. While both tell of Honoria's consent to be Felix's bride and his twinge of disappointment that the queenly angel he has worshiped should lower herself to join with him, the later version emphasizes her submissiveness, the earlier version her companionable presence. In 1886, that is, the book closes when

The mistress of my reverent thought,
  Whose praise was all I ask'd of fame,
In my close-watch'd approval sought
  Protection as from danger and blame;
Her soul, which late I loved to invest
  With pity for my poor desert,
Buried its face within my breast,
  Like a pet fawn by hunters hurt.
(1886:137)

The same lines appear in the 1854 poem, but they are not the final word. They are followed by a section in which Felix finds himself wishing Honoria loved him less, since she dismays him by making him "her lord," but he realizes the error of this response (1854:182). The poem then concludes with a final section. Here Felix may still be lord, but the two lovers sit side by side rather than assuming the tableau of a cowering Honoria who buries her face against a mastering male:

I buried soon, in the deep sea
  Of a most near and dear content,
All pride and all humility:
  So she beside me sat her down,
Excused from dignity and care,
  And I submitted to the crown
No choice was left me but to wear.
(1854:183)

Nor does the volume end there. As opposed to the 1886 version, which ends with the image of the trembling pet fawn, the 1854 poem reverts to the outer frame. The wife praises the husband's work, and he reads her the beginning of the second book when she interrupts. Though her objection is based on prudery, she *does* interrupt, feeling free to intrude her own voice and vision at will:

But here his Wife,
  All praise till now, objected: "This,"
Said she, "you did not take from life:
  "You should not make the [betrothed] lady kiss."

The fault confess'd with light demur,
  Those lines he promised to remove,
Fixing in colloquy with her,
  [The] canons of their Court of Love.
(1854:189–90)

The 1854 volume ends, that is, with the wife again established as her husband's collaborator. With a single significant exception,[8] the same pattern characterizes *The Espousals*, published (also anonymously) in 1856. Here, too, the woman is a more active participant in life, love, and poetry than she is in the final version of 1886. Numerous passages in which her words appear, for example, were removed by the time Patmore fixed the final text. Even in the Prologue, the frame which appears in both versions, the woman's words are presented in 1856, silenced in 1886. In response to her husband's praise of her beauty, she *voices* her reply in 1856, with banter that playfully challenges her husband's sally: "She laughs and says, 'Twere always so / Were all wives loved as he loves her" (1856:4). But in the final version she merely looks dumbly on: "Bright looks reply, approving so / Beauty's elixir vitae, praise" (1886:138).

Honoria's voice is also diminished in the poem proper as we turn from the 1856 to the 1886 edition. The eighth canto of the 1886 poem, "The Koh-i-noor," begins with Felix setting forth his ideal of the womanly mind at Honoria's request. This passage served as Accompaniment to the eleventh idyl in the 1856 poem—the accompaniments in general being more abstract and didactic (hence less appealing to twentieth-century minds) than the narrative cantos which more easily follow the path of unideal life.[9] Here is the opening of the 1886 canto:

Be man's hard virtues highly wrought,
  But let my gentle Mistress be,
In every look, word, deed, and thought,
  Nothing but sweet and womanly!
Her virtues please my virtuous mood,
  But what at all times I admire
Is, not that she is wise or good,
  But just the thing which I desire.

With versatility to sing
 The theme of love to any strain,
If oft'nest she is anything,
 Be it careless, talkative, and vain.
That seems in her supremest grace
 Which, virtue or not, apprises me
That my familiar thoughts embrace
 Unfathomable mystery.
(1886:183)

It is startling to see, in contrast, the corresponding section of the 1856 poem, an idyl entitled "Tete-A-Tete," that is, two heads close together and communicating rather than an inert object of great value. In this idyl the apostrophe to sharply distinct sex roles gives way to an amusingly unideal and chatty scene between the two lovers in which Felix is initiated into the finer points of garment construction:[10]

"What's this?" "Miss Gussett's Fashion-Book.
 "Do you like flounc'd or plain skirts best?"
"O, flounc'd, like your's. These—"
 "gathers" "look
"Too straight: I like them thus, recess'd."
"That fashion's old." "You've charming taste
 "In colours: dim grey with a dash
"Of gayest azure at the waist!
 "How I should like to have that sash!
"Oh, thanks. What narrow boundaries hold
 "My world! You are so fair—but, Dear,
"You must be tired of being told?"
 "Oh, no, Love!" "Are you pleased to hear?"
"I would, of course, seem fair to you."
 "But, Sweetest, you must promise me
"To think my praises simply true!"
(1856:100–101)[11]

Honoria not only gets to speak more (though in quoted form) in 1856; she is also a more active participant in love. When the married couple of the prologue compare their current joy with that of courtship, the 1886 poem states that only the man had wooed in early days: "They blest the days they had been wed, / At cost of those in which he woo'd" (1886:139). But the 1856 couple remember a reciprocal process: "They praised the days that they'd been wed, / At cost of those in which they woo'd" (1856:139). An even more poignant instance occurs in the poem's tenth idyl, called, in 1856, "The Eve of the Wedding" ("The Epitaph," in 1886). In the first edition the sole Accompaniment to the idyl, called "The Meditation," breaks Patmore's usual pattern and presents a narrative rather than a lyric. The verse gives a sympathetic, sensitive account of a woman's fears on the eve of her wedding. The oblique reference to fears about the woman's first sexual experience testifies to what could become, as Phyllis Rose argues in *Parallel Lives*,[12] the trauma of the wedding night for the sexually uninitiated:

> She sits upon her little bed,
>   And muses by the musing moon:
> Ere this to-morrow she'll be wed!
>   Ere this? Ere this? How strangely soon!
> An obvious blank of ignorance
>   Lies full across her forward way,
> And shadows, cast from unknown chance,
>   Make strange and dim the coming day.
> She must not muse too much! Vague fear
>   O'erfilms her apprehensive eye;
> And she may swoon, with no one near,
>   And haply so, unmarried, die.
> Her faithless dread she now discards;
>   And now remorseful memory flings
> Its glory round the last
>   Of home and old accustom'd things.
> (1856:137–38)

The second section of "The Meditation" then recounts her fears about leaving her parents and suffering the diminishment of her husband's love—"Ah, should her lover's love abate; / And should she, miserable, lose / All dear regards of maiden state, / Dissolved by time and marriage dues" (1856:139). In the end she summons the resolution to banish her fears, but the length and intensity with which her fears are articulated answer to her fiancé's similar fears recounted in the idyl proper:

> Vague discontents awaken'd, fed
> By wealth exceeding hope or aim,
> And fears, like Salamanders, bred
> In love's so long unfaltering flame:
> Ah, what if time should make us twain,
> Or course of custom let us run,
> With undistinguish'd heart and brain,
> Like neighbouring dew-drops into one?
> Or what if love were blind? Then she,
> This maid, who now appear'd most rare,
> When time had taught my heart to see,
> Might prove less worshipfully fair.
> If not, then I, found little worth,
> Might drop ridiculously down
> From love's heroic height to earth,
> And cast my sceptre and my crown.
> (1856:145)

Although the 1886 poem also alludes to the bridegroom's fears the night before the wedding, the specific doubts of the 1856 poem were entirely excised, and the remaining doubts left vague and inconsequential. Even more was lost, however, in cutting "The Meditation," which imparts greater humanity to the bride, and shared emotions to bride and bridegroom. They both love, they both fear in 1856; in 1886 the groom loves and desires, the bride is a silent object of desire.

As the 1856 bride is less silent, so is the 1856 wife, who is granted, as in 1854, a share in the poem being produced. Both the 1856 and 1886 versions of *The Espousals* come to a close when Felix and Honoria marry and begin their honeymoon; an Epilogue then recurs to the mature married couple of the frame narrative. In 1886 the Epilogue begins with the poet's assertion of his role as poet:

> 'Ah, dearest Wife, a fresh-lit fire
> 'Sends forth to heaven great shows of fume,

'And watchers, far away, admire;
  'But when the flames their power assume,
'The more they burn the less they show,
  'The clouds no longer smirch the sky,
'And then the flames intensest glow
  'When far-off watchers think they die.
'The fumes of early love my verse
  'Has figured—'
(1886:205–6)

In 1856 the Epilogue begins with the wife's critique of the poem she has just heard:

"I did not call you 'Dear' or 'Love,'
  "I think, till after Frank was born."
"That fault I cannot well remove;
"The rhymes"—But Frank now blew his horn
(1856:177)

And general domestic chaos ensues. The same passage occurs in the 1886 poem, but only after the male poet has spoken. Moreover, the 1886 husband refuses the wife's request that the poem continue; when the wife pleads that the husband "paint the flame" of married love, he dismisses her request, rejoining, "''Twould merit the Promethean curse!'" (1886:206). The 1856 poem depicts a different outcome:

"The fumes of early love my verse
  "Hath figured, but to paint the flame
"Might merit the Promethean curse,
  "And is a task unknown to fame."—
"The task you undertook was such:
  "Do, Dear, go on!"—and he, who cried,
"'I could not love thee, Muse, so much
  "'Loved I not Honor more!'" complied.
(1856:181)

Certainly the fact that Patmore did not finish the poem explains the deletion of this passage in 1886. Still, the earlier volume as a whole displays a different attitude toward the wife's participation in a poem so closely tied to the married love she also shares. Hence the 1856 volume ends, as the 1886 version does not, with a two-way conversation on poetry: "they [not he] talk'd of olden song" (1856:181). I do not suggest that the first two parts of *Angel in the House* possess in their original form an innocence of ideology or disinterested commitment to women—far from it. Yet it is significant that the earlier version so often grants the major female figure a vitality and presence denied her in the authorized version.

In the 1860 installment Honoria and Felix appear but are no longer the major focus of the narrative. *Faithful for Ever,* an epistolary volume, tells the story of Frederick Graham, the cousin and disappointed suitor of Honoria (he briefly appears in the *Betrothal* and *Espousals*), and Jane, the chaplain's daughter he marries for solace after Honoria weds Felix. Theirs is a story of ordinary, not ethereal and idealized love, and the earthiness of tone and situation form strong contrasts to *The Betrothal* and *The Espousals.* Once again there are significant differences between the first and authorized editions, one of which is format. The first edition is divided into three sections: Book I, "Honoria"; Book II, "Jane"; and Book III, "Rachel"; no division occurs in the 1886 work, which is an uninterrupted sequence of nineteen letters. More important, in the first edition Jane is accorded more dignity and is more clearly an earthly double of Honoria, who resurfaces in distinctly mundane form in 1860. In later editions, characteristically, Patmore more strongly emphasized women as idealized icons who bear the impress of male needs and desires.

The book devoted to Honoria, which presents her as the refined, gracious, angelic presence Frederick yearns for but does not quite achieve (or deserve), changed little from the first to the last edition. But the 1860 and 1886 texts reveal clear distinctions in the handling of Book II, devoted to Jane. In revising the "letters" which follow Jane's introduction to the narrative, Patmore regrettably backed away from what was perhaps his freshest character (if one still forced to unfold within strict bounds). When Frederick writes his mother in the 1886 volume to inform her that he has married, Jane's gracelessness and obtuse passivity are underlined in the marriage "proposal":

> knowing that *she* could not care,
> I turn'd away from my despair,
> And told our chaplain's daughter, Jane,—
> A dear, good girl, who saw my pain,
> And look'd as if she pitied me,—
> How glad and thankful I should be
> If some kind woman, not above
> Myself in rank, would give her love
> To one that knew not how to woo.
> Whereat she, without more ado,
> Blush'd, spoke of love return'd, and closed
> With what she thought I had proposed.
> (1886:248)

In this passage Jane is silent, able only to "look" her thoughts, until she misinterprets Fred's words and blurts out a proposal. In 1860 Jane is still decidedly lower in class than Frederick, but she speaks her thoughts instead of passively "looking" them, and she is more acute about Fred's intentions:

> knowing that *she* could not care,
> I turn'd my back on my despair;
> And told our chaplain's daughter, Jane,—
> A dear, good Girl, who saw my pain,
> And spoke as if she pitied me,—
> How glad and thankful I should be
> If some kind woman, not above
> Myself in rank, would give her love
> To one that knew not how to woo.
> Whereat she, without more ado,
> Blush'd, spoke of love return'd, and closed
> With what I meant to have proposed.
> (1860:100–101)

One 1886 revision, it is true, imparts greater dignity to Jane rather than the reverse. In 1860 the letter above was followed by one from Jane to Mrs. Graham, a letter Fred ordered Jane to write, and one apparently intended by Patmore to stamp vulgarity upon Jane in every line. The following passage, in which Jane invites her new mother-in-law to visit, is representative: "The house is rather small we've got, / But dear Fred says that yours is not / So large by half; so you'll not mind" (1860:116). Jane is also singularly imperceptive in this letter, not guessing that the angel Fred mentions is Honoria, not his mother: "If I bewail our nature's taint, / He says he has seen a faultless Saint. / Of course that's you" (1860:117). The only saving grace of the letter is the foreshadowing of Jane's own eventual grace to Fred, an agency of which she is as yet unaware: "I have hopes of him; for, oh, / How can we ever surely know / But that the very darkest place / May be the scene of saving grace, / Which softens even hearts of stone!" (1860:118). At this point Jane herself is that "darkest place," and Patmore's removal of the offensive letter is an uncommon instance of his granting more rather than less to a female character through his revisions.

As with the volumes of the 1850s, the female heroine (in this case, Jane) more actively inhabits her body than does the more symbolic counterpart of the final version. Thus the first edition of *Faithful for Ever* contains references to pregnancy, the suckling of a child, and the unaesthetic realities of physical illness; all were cut from the final version.[13] But the most significant difference between the two versions lies not in the contents of individual sections but in the larger structuring of the epistles. Both the 1860 and 1886 poems begin with a section devoted to Fred's idealized, unrequited love for Honoria, followed by letters recounting Fred's rash marriage to Jane, the initial strain in their relation, and their warming toward each other with the birth of their first child. Only minor disparities exist between the 1860 and 1886 contents of these sections.

But the third section ("Rachel" in 1860, a section of only three letters in 1886) is radically different in the earlier versus later poem. "Rachel" is structured to narrate Jane's social and domestic triumph and her kinship with Honoria. At the outset of "Rachel" Honoria visits the Graham household after being in the neighborhood and hearing that Fred is ill with fever. Jane and Honoria (partly, we are to see, because of Honoria's graciousness) immediately like each other, and Jane accepts Honoria's invitation to visit the Vaughans. Fred, hearing this, grows red and refuses, an indication that his heart is not yet free from Honoria's lure, though he is now the father of a child by Jane. The next letter in "Rachel," set four years later, is from Honoria's youngest sister, Lady Clitheroe, recounting Fred and Jane's visit to Honoria and Felix's estate. Though "outré" in so many ways, Jane is a great success with the county squirearchy and other notables, who consider her charming (though Jane wishes she could be as graceful as Honoria, whom she greatly admires). Indeed, so fetching is Jane that Honoria actually grows jealous: Jane is the only other woman who has been able to attract Felix, and Honoria declares she must not have Jane visiting too often. Fred, too, now sees enhanced charms in Jane, and by this time his love for Honoria has merged with his strong love for Jane. The last two letters of the section (and the volume) then describe the celebration of Fred and Jane's twelfth wedding anniversary, first from Fred's point of view, then from Jane's, whose voice and vision thus become the end point to which the entire volume has led. If, sadly, her proof that Fred now cares so greatly for her is that he grows more tyrannical, insisting that she take care of herself, the improvement in their relationship is indicated by his impulsively kissing her foot out of love and their discussing together the finer points of theology. This is the first anniversary they have ever celebrated formally, and the fine June day, shaken by storms only to subside into dewy coolness, is an apt analogue of the more fruitful relation (if one lacking passion) at which they have arrived after initial misery and upheaval.

In addition to charting the progress of a marriage and Jane's increasing social success, the structuring of the 1860 "Rachel" suggests the close ties of Jane and Honoria, who emerge as doubles.[14] Both ultimately inspire the admiration of Felix and the love of Fred. Though their alignment can be put to symbolic use (one representing the spiritual side of woman or marriage, one the earthly), this relation also suggests new facets of the women's characters. While Jane's success (which, within the conservative ideology of the poem, consists of ingratiating the upper class and pleasing men) is seen partly as a result of her marriage and her interactions with social superiors, her triumphant manifestation of self at the Vaughans' also suggests that the seeds of her charm and graciousness were there all along and have simply developed over time. Honoria similarly upholds traditional, conservative values, but the single instance in which she speaks in her own voice is a deliberately de-idealizing one. All along, her letter suggests, she has been more than the heavenly icon celebrated by Felix (whose voice and point of view are firmly excluded from this volume), for she was also an earthly and earth-bound woman with her own voice. Since virtually no traces of it remain in the better-known version of Patmore's poem, her letter to her father is quoted in full below:

> Dearest Papa, at last we are come,
> The tiresome season over, home!
> How honourable it seems to me!
> I am sick of town society,
> The Opera, and the flatteries
> Of cynic, disrespectful eyes!
>   Frederick is here. Tell Mrs. Fife;
> Who adored him. He has brought his wife.
> She *is* so nice; but Felix goes
> Next Sunday with her to the Close
> And you will judge her. She the first
> Has made me jealous, though the Hurst
> Is lit so oft with loveliness,
> And, when in town, where I was less
> Constrain'd in choice, I always ask'd
> The prettiest. Felix really bask'd
> Like Puss in fire-shine, when the room
> Was all aflame with female bloom;
> And, since I praised and did not pout,
> His little, lawless loves went out
> With the last brocade. 'Tis not the same,
> I find, with Mrs. Frederick Graham!

I must not have her stopping here
More than a fortnight once a year.
My husband says he never saw
Such proof of what he holds for law
That beauty is love which can be seen.
Whatever he by this may mean,
Were it not fearful if he fell
In love with her on principle!
  Felix has spoken only twice [in Parliament]:
Once on Savoy, and once on this
Shameful Reform Bill; and on each
He made a most successful speech;
And both times I, of course, was there
And heard him cheer'd. But, (how unfair!)
Whenever, wishing to explain
His meaning, he got up again,
They call'd out "Order" and "Oh, oh!"
He abused the Newspapers, and so
The "Times" left out the cries of "hear."
The very Opposition cheer
Dear Felix; and at what he said
The Arch-Radical turn'd white and red.
I saw him with my opera-glass.
Yet they allow'd the law to pass
The second reading. Should this cheat
Succeed next spring, we lose our seat!
Nor shall I grieve. The wisest say
There's near at hand an evil day;
And, though, if Felix chose to stir,
I am sure he might be Minister,
I tell him, they serve England most
Who keep, at whatsoever cost,
Their honour; and, when best and first
Have flung their strength to last and worst,
And ruling means, from hour to hour
Cajoling those who have the power,
A gentleman should stay at home,
And let his rulers sometimes come

And blush at his high privacy.
Felix, I know, agrees with me,
Although he calls me, "Fierce white cat!"
And says, 'tis not yet come to that.
  Yesterday, he and I fell out;
Can you believe it? 'Twas about
The cost at which he says I dress'd
Last season. I came off the best;[15]
And you, Papa, by both stand task'd
Instead, as you shall learn: I ask'd,
Would he, at one house, think it nice
To see me in the same dress twice?
Of course he kiss'd me, and said, "No!"
And then I proved, *he* made me go
To Lady Lidderdale's three fetes
And both her dances! *Magistrates*
Ought to know better than to try
a charge dismiss'd; and he and I
Had talk'd this over once before!
Forgiv'n, he vow'd to offend no more.
But, oh, he actually says
You caution'd him against my ways.
We both are shock'd Papa could be
So cruel and unfatherly!
(1860:195–99)

Notable in this letter are Honoria's patronizing of Felix (rather than the reverse) on the matter of his flirtations with belles, her assumption that Felix agrees with her on political principles rather than the reverse, and their arguing which culminates, according to Honoria, in her besting her husband.

Of course the letter is distastefully coy and explicitly reactionary, but for my purposes here the significant thing is that it exists at all, and that it makes of Honoria an ordinary, nonsymbolic woman rather than a symbolic angel who inspires men. This letter appalled Patmore's readers, at least his male readers,[16] and this is surely one reason he removed the letter in later editions. But the removal of the letter also weakens the link between Honoria and Jane and hence undermines a major point of the 1860 volume.

In fact the 1886 version destroys almost every point made in the 1860 "Rachel" section. Honoria's letter is wholly cut, and as a result she never speaks in her own voice in the entire *Angel in the House*. Instead Felix's voice is brought into the seventeenth letter of "Faithful for Ever" (from a letter originally placed midway through the *Macmillan's Magazine Victories of Love* published in late 1861.) Writing during a brief absence from home, he apostrophizes Honoria and their love in terms that re-establish idealized, frankly poetic love as the value center against which Fred and Jane's love must be set and found less beautiful and grand. An account of the Grahams' eighth (rather than twelfth) anniversary immediately follows, where it can attain maximum contrast with the love of Felix and Honoria. This rearrangement also means that the anniversary is no longer the point, the achievement, toward which the whole of *Faithful for Ever* leads but a stopping place on the way to the actual climax of the book. That climax comes in the next epistle (the nineteenth), which tells of Honoria's visit, the invitation to stay with the Vaughans, Fred's refusal of the invitation, and Jane's response:

> Dear Fred wrote,
> Directly, such a lovely note,
> Which, though it undid all I had done,
> Was, both to me and Mrs. Vaughan,
> So kind! His words, I can't say why,
> Like soldiers' music, made me cry.
> (1886:273)

The 1860 volume had ended with Jane's confident assurance of Fred's love as they celebrate their anniversary following her social triumph. Here she is left to cry after having Fred thwart her wishes, and in context the passage suggests that Fred refuses because he is still enamoured of Honoria and so cannot trust himself to pay an extended visit. This volume splits the alignment of Jane and Honoria and clearly elevates the more etherealized, symbolic character over the mundane Jane.

Indeed, Jane is allowed to visit the Vaughans only in the

"Victories of Love" section in the 1886 poem, and by then the visit is a consolation prize for the fact that her two youngest children have died and she is herself in the early stages of mortal illness (her description of the visit to the Vaughan estate now concludes with a reference to her persistent cough [1886:283]). Once again the effect is to disembody a female character, yoke her to a symbolic function, and, in addition, literally entomb her, since Jane is dead by the seventh letter in the 1886 Book II. She marries, teaches Fred the meaning of love that grows from lowly beginnings and develops over time, and then efficiently dies. She is denied an unalloyed personal triumph, since now her presence at the Vaughans', though still a winning one, is tinged with pathos. She is denied a healthy, serene celebration of her anniversary after a visit whose duration she (in 1860), not Fred, controls; she is even denied some of her conversations with Fred. A major portion of the 1860 passage in which Fred discusses theology with Jane on their anniversary becomes, in the 1886 poem, part of a letter Fred writes to Honoria after Jane's death. Fred, to be sure, realizes even before Jane dies that he loves her profoundly, but Jane now seems to exist for the sake of this revelation and for her role in conveying a paradigm of marriage rather than for her existence as an embodied person who merits attention as a human being.

To discuss the first versus later edition of *Victories of Love* is a more complicated matter because two editions can claim to be part of the first serial edition. The earliest version appeared in the October, November, and December issues of *Macmillan's Magazine* in 1861. But the bound volume which appeared with rearranged contents in 1863 was also issued *as* a part or installment of the larger series, as indicated in Patmore's endnote quoted above. Both contrast in significant ways with the 1886 authorized version, which in fact merged *Faithful for Ever* and *Victories of Love.*

Victories of Love also complicates matters because the pattern evident in the treatment of major female characters is less consistent than in Patmore's revisions of earlier parts. In both the 1861 and 1863 versions there is an extended passage on the doctrine of wifely submission which was trimmed, not expanded, in the 1886 poem.[17] And the 1861 magazine edition (the "first" first edition) is in some ways less kind to women than the volume issued in 1863. Though the serial format meant that Jane's triumph at the end of *Faithful for Ever* could exist in the audience's minds for a year or more before the next part appeared, the 1861 *Victories* began with a death knell for Jane: "Dear Mother, I can surely tell, / Now, that I never shall get well" (Oct. 1861:436). The overall pattern of the 1861 poem is emphatically a paradigm of entombment: it begins with Jane's mortal illness and quickly moves to her death, signaled by the second letter, since this and the two succeeding letters are to be read only after her death ("this I've written to be read / To comfort you when I am dead" [Oct. 1861:439]). The first four letters thus concern her death and the status of the Grahams' love after she is dead. In the fifth, Mary Churchill explains to her father why she spurns marriage altogether, and in the sixth, Felix writes to Honoria in honor of their twentieth anniversary. The last three sections of the 1861 poem concern the wedding of John Graham with Emily Vaughan, culminating in the wedding sermon preached by Dean Churchill. While this wedding is a comic renewal that enables the various loves of Felix, Honoria, Frederick, and Jane to go on in modified guise,[18] the beginning and end of the 1861 poem stress disembodied or spiritual-symbolic love: we begin with a character's death and end with a sermon stressing the metaphysical interpretation of the marriage bond. There is a fine logic to this arrangement: the placement of Felix's letter indicates that the mature marital bliss he continues to enjoy with Honoria is a gradation in a sequence from newlywed love to love transcending death, and a worthy counterpart to the virginal piety of Mary. But the Jane who was so triumphant at the end of *Faithful for Ever* is drained of all presence and is put to symbolic use from the beginning of the sequence.

The 1863 volume is kinder to Jane, especially as a sequel to her trip to High Hurst and her serene anniversary celebration with Fred. The 1863 volume begins and ends with Felix and Honoria's love. Insofar as their love is still idealized and Honoria a beloved icon, the pattern here is also one of entombment (that is, of emptying a female figure of life in favor of status as a symbolic object). But at least Jane's death is postponed in this version and earthly love given more emphasis than love in death. The 1863 volume opens with Felix's letter to Honoria during a brief absence from home (the letter which, in 1886, became the seventeenth letter in "Faithful for Ever"), reestablishing, after the absence of Felix's voice in 1860, idealized but now maturing rather than static love as a frame of reference. There follows a letter from Jane to her mother telling of the deaths of Grace and the baby (last seen in the closing letter of the 1860 *Faithful*) and articulating the doctrine of wifely submission. But there is as yet no hint of illness in Jane. Only the third letter involves Jane in death; there follow, as in 1861, the letters she writes to be read after her death. Immediately after the last of these, however, in which she foretells John and Emily's marriage, Lady Clitheroe describes that marriage, so that Jane's prophecy is fulfilled. Then come Mary Churchill's letter celebrating the chaste life, a worldly letter of marital advice from Lady Clitheroe to newlywed Emily, the wedding sermon which Mary has copied out for Emily, and the culmination to which all has led, Felix's letter to Honoria on their twentieth anniversary. Honoria continues more iconic than real, more desired object than person, but the point to which this volume builds is the shared achievement of a developing and still-growing relationship that has already endured twenty years. And this ending also celebrates the poem which has been growing over the years as well. The letter opens, "Dearest, my Love and Wife, 'tis long / Ago I closed the unfinish'd song / Which never could be finish'd."[19] And at the end Felix asserts that while England in the future might lose its prestige, it will still be remembered for harboring a poet who took as his subject marital love. As he imagines a future reader saying:

> "Great is the Land that somewhat best
> Works, to the wonder of the rest!
> We, in our day, have better done
> This thing or that than any one;
> And who but, still admiring, sees

How excellent for images
Was Greece, for laws how wise was Rome;
But read this Poet, and say if home
And private love did e'er so smile
As in that ancient English Isle!"
(1863:104)

In contrast to this celebration of developing love, marriage, and poetry, the 1886 "Victories of Love" opens and closes with versions of the same letters that begin and end the *Macmillan's* 1861 *Victories*. Not only does the final version thus revert to the entombment paradigm but it also diminishes (as noted above) Jane's social success and marital fulfillment. Moreover, the final lines to the wedding sermon no longer stress continued (if spiritual-symbolic) growth of love, as they did in 1861:

Have you not seen a bird's beak slay
Proud Psyche, on a summer's day?
Down fluttering drop the frail wings four,
Wanting the weight that made them soar!
Spirit is heavy Nature's wing,
And is not rightly anything
Without its burthen, whereas this,
Wingless, at least a maggot is,
And, wing'd, is honour and delight
Increasing endlessly with height.
(Dec. 1861:119)

The final, 1886 version added to this a passage adapted from Dean Churchill's letter to Frederick in the 1860 *Faithful*, stating the function of ideal, unattainable love (an obvious reference to Fred's passion for Honoria):

Then was that nought,
That trance of joy beyond all thought,
The vision, in one, of womanhood?
Nay, for all women holding good,
Should marriage such a prologue want
'Twere sordid and most ignorant
Profanity; but, having this,

'Tis honour now, and future bliss;
For where is he that, knowing the height
And depth of ascertain'd delight,
Inhumanly henceforward lies
Content with mediocrities!
(1886:337)

The final word is not about continued growth upward but about the absolute value of a beloved icon. A process has been replaced by a static object.

What, then, is the significance of Patmore's revisions as a whole? Certainly the revisions tend to verify Patmore's claim in the endnote to the 1863 *Victories* that Emily Patmore was essential to his composition of the poem.[20] Her immediate presence and, after July 5, 1862, when she died, the immediate memory of her helped preserve traces of an active, earthly, female human being in the poem, one with a mind and voice of her own.[21] By the time Patmore established the final reading of the poem in 1886 he was twenty-four years and two wives away from Emily. Perhaps not surprisingly, the 1886 poem increasingly severs its links with an active female presence and celebrates the eternal feminine, passive and silent, rather than the mortal woman.

But this pattern of revision is also significant because it accords with the pattern of "Romantic revision" identified by Charles Rosen, which tends to move "away from direct experience to a mediated reflection."[22] In fact Rosen provides an instance of revision quite similar to Patmore's. As Rosen argues, the female character in Balzac's *Le Chef d'oeuvre inconnu,* first serialized in the 1831 issues of *L'Artiste* before appearing in volume form in 1837, was a "creature" in the first edition, a "creation" in the second: "In the 1831 version, the living being takes precedence over the made object. By 1837 Balzac's hubris has increased, and the work of art is nobler than the woman."[23] What the first editions of Patmore's *Angel in the House* and Balzac's *Unknown Masterpiece* have in common is that they were serials; that is, both authors were involved in an ongoing relation with their own artworks in these works' first appearances. Indeed, the prologue to the 1856 *Espousals* (in a passage later cut) inscribes the reception of the first volume and shows the poet vulnerably poised between censure and praise:

> the wish'd-for post-bag, [was] fill'd,
> Like Fame's puff'd cheek, with Vaughan's success.
> A letter from the Laureate thrill'd
> Her voice that read it; but the Press,
> Daily and weekly, death-notes toll'd:
> Some call'd him harsh, but full of fire,
> Some call'd him musical, but cold;
> And earn'd his wife's contempt and ire.
> He laugh'd; but, seeing his Poem named
> With Holofernes Brobdignag,
> And nine new Miltons more, exclaim'd,
> With patience that began to flag,
> "I, servant to the Truth in times
> "When gaudy words are more than wit,
> "And diligent in all my rhymes
> "The truth with truest phrase to fit,
> "Am unsolicitous to earn
> "Mock laurels, and amaze with show
> "The vulgar, who will nothing learn
> "But that which they already know.
> "Yet Love, requiring language high
> "Beyond our tongue's extremest reach,
> "May class me, to the careless eye,
> "With modern mountebanks of speech:
> "But we'll our hearts in patience keep,
> "Till this indignity be past,
> "Sure that the worthless oyster-heap
> "Shall waste, and show the pearls at last."
> (1856:4–6)

Not only were both Patmore and Balzac involved in a living relation with their serial compositions; both authors also more clearly articulated in their serials than in their single-volume editions relations between a man and a *living* woman. When each artist finished his first version of the artwork and returned to it as an object which could be changed, modified, and manipulated to achieve greater refinement and beauty *as* an object, the women in both works became increasingly emptied of vitality and presence and likewise acquired a status more closely identified with a beautiful object.

It is good to be able to say that Patmore's first impulse in the poem was often more generous to women than his final and considered gesture. His case, however, like Balzac's, suggests issues that go beyond Romanticism. Patmore's revisions remind us of the semantic relation between the words "author," "authority," "authoritative," and "authorized." In *Angel in the House* there is a relation between increasing control of the text and increasing control over the female image.[24] Perhaps in authors so disposed by temperament, history, and ideology, a masterpiece, finished to the last detail, is a piece of mastery indeed, a piece in which control over the text becomes associated with control over women (or any variant of the other). In the case of *Angel in the House,* preferring the first, serial edition to the final, authorized edition can help readers to recover a poem less distasteful to twentieth-century sensibilities and effectively to resist a control that is expressed over the body of the text and the body of the female. It may not be possible (or desirable) to revive the angel entombed in the poem, but we can at least discover the living presence that first death, then the poet's revisions, encased in silence.

NOTES

1. Jerome J. McGann, "The Monks and the Giants: Textual and Bibliographical Studies and the Interpretation of Literary Works," in *Textual Criticism and Literary Interpretation,* ed. Jerome J. McGann (Chicago and London: University of Chicago Press, 1985), pp. 180–99.

2. E. J. Oliver, *Coventry Patmore* (New York: Sheed & Ward, 1956), p. 168; Mario Praz, *The Hero in Eclipse in Victorian Fiction,* trans. Angus Davidson (London: Oxford University Press, 1956), p. 440, n. 15.

3. Edmund Gosse, *Coventry Patmore* (London: Hodder & Stoughton, 1905), pp. 66–68; Sister Mary Anthony Weinig, *Coventry Patmore* (Boston: Twayne, 1981), p. 75.

4. Basil Champneys, *Memoirs and Correspondence of Coventry Patmore,* 2 vols. (London: George Bell & Sons, 1900), 2:186–87.

5. Weinig, p. 137, n. 12.

6. Coventry Patmore, *The Poems of Coventry Patmore,* ed. Frederick Page (London: Oxford University Press, 1949). Although all citations (by page number) are from Page's 1949 edition, the 1886 date is used, since this indicates the date the actual text was established. All lines from the poem's first edition are also cited by date and page number. The parts of the first edition include: Patmore, *The Angel in the House: The Betrothal* (London: J. W. Parker & Son, 1854); *The Angel in the House: The Espousals* (London: J. W. Parker & Son, 1856); *Faithful for Ever* (London: J. Parker & Son, 1860); "The Victories of Love," *Macmillan's Magazine* 4 (October 1861): 436–48; 5 (November, December 1861): 23–37, 109–119; *The Victories of Love* (London and Cambridge: Macmillan, 1863).

7. Carol T. Christ identifies this lyric as a key passage, one which reveals that the assertions about sexual difference developed in the poem derive from male anxiety about sexuality (Carol T. Christ, "Victorian Masculinity and the Angel in the House," in *A Widening Sphere: Changing Roles of Victorian Women,* ed. Martha Vicinus [Bloomington: Indiana University Press, 1977], pp. 146–62).

8. In the section entitled "The Love Letters" (Idyl 5 in 1856, Canto 6 in 1886), both versions have an initial letter sent from Felix to Honoria, then Honoria's reply to Felix. The 1886 canto ends there, giving Honoria the last word and emphasizing their reciprocal communication. The 1856 idyl, however, adds another letter from Felix to Honoria, one which overlays her own and which decidedly emphasizes the beloved as object (an "Ark") rather than as living presence: "You are to me the only Ark / Of that high mystery which locks / The lips of joy, or speaks in dark / Enigmas and in paradox" (1856:76). From here the letter continues into ever more airy and idealizing regions, until the woman's humanity is entirely lost. This instance suggests, of course, the dangers of absolute generalizations in writerly patterns and perhaps also reminds us that Patmore, too, is more than a reified, predictable object.

9. A similar occurrence can be found in Canto 4 of the 1886 poem (entitled "Love in Idleness"). The concluding narrative section of the canto is actually adapted from an accompaniment in the 1854 *Betrothal* (the third accompaniment to Idyl 8). The analogous section to "Love in Idleness" in the 1856 *Espousals* is the idyl entitled "The Regatta," and here the narrative proper ends with dialogue—with, that is, a sustained focus on story rather than on lyric reflection.

10. What Patricia Ball remarks of *The Betrothal* is true here as well, for she asserts that the cantos of *The Betrothal* show "how the daily minutiae and the fundamentals of loving relate to each other" (Patricia Ball, *The Heart's Events: The Victorian Poetry of Relationships* [London: University of London Athlone Press, 1976], p. 197).

11. Patmore also cut several lines quoting Honoria's words from the second and eleventh idyls of the 1856 poem.

12. Phyllis Rose, *Parallel Lives: Five Victorian Marriages* (New York: Vintage, 1984), pp. 55–60.

13. See 1856:132–33, 148, 168–69. As Jane writes in the first passage,

"Mother, I look and feel so ill; / And soon I shall be uglier still, / You know. But I have heard that men / Never think women ugly then. / Pray write and tell me if that's true."

14. See Hughes and Lund for a further discussion of this point (Linda K. Hughes and Michael Lund, *The Victorian Serial* [forthcoming]).

15. The 1856 volume had carefully prepared for this line. In Idyl 11 the Dean had said to his new son-in-law, "Watch, by the way, or else she'll spend / Too much in alms-deed and on dress" (1856:157). A letter from Lady Clitheroe in the 1860 volume makes it clear Honoria uses money allotted for clothes to give to the poor:

> Though all confess
> Her tact is absolute in dress,
> She does not get her things so *good*
> As, with her fortune now, she should.
> I feel quite certain, between us,
> She cheats her husband, (she did thus
> With her dear Papa,) and has no end
> Of pin-money, full half to spend
> On folks who think themselves in this
> Paid takers of her tolls to Bliss.
> (1860:180–81)

16. Basil Champneys records Dr. Richard Garnett's pained reaction to Honoria's epistle after reading a draft of *Faithful for Ever* prior to publication:

> I must admit that Honoria's re-appearance in the third book is indispensable; but for heaven's sake let us have as little of her domestic arrangements as may be, and I would certainly advise you to expunge her letter to the Dean. This has, in my eyes, the double fault of contributing nothing whatever to the progress of the story, and of quite failing to confirm the idea of the lady we have been led to form from the enthusiastic idea of her love. Frankly, it is the poorest passage of the poem, and Honoria's taking up the pen for the first and last time to write *it* reminds me rather forcibly of Coleridge's anecdote of the silent man and the apple dumplings. (Champneys, *Memoirs*, 2:343–44)

Champneys himself also expresses relief that the letter was cut (Ibid., 1:174–75). See Hughes and Lund for example of reaction to the 1860 volume in published reviews.

17. See October 1861: 438–39 and 1863: 14–17.

18. See also Weinig, p. 78.

19. 1863:90. See Hughes and Lund for a further discussion of the analogue between the theme of marriage and the poem's serial publication format.

20. E. J. Oliver makes the interesting observation that "this poem has in it a physical and moral comfort such as [Emily Patmore] provided in his daily life. She soothed and to some extent suppressed some of his most characteristic impulses" (Oliver, p. 47).

21. Though she confined her efforts to domestic management and children's verse, Emily Patmore was herself the author of two published books (see Champneys, 1:120).

22. Charles Rosen, "Romantic Originals," *New York Review of Books* 22 (17 December 1987): 24.

23. Ibid., p. 22.

24. James Parins suggestively notes that "Patmore believed that authority and form begin in law, and that joy, beauty and excellence in art, as well as love, proceed from underlying laws which govern the nature of both" (James W. Parins, "Poetic Calculus: Patmore's Parabolic Vocabulary," *Victorians Institute Journal* 6 [1977]: 49–66).

11

Conrad, *Under Western Eyes*, and the Mysteries of Revision*

David Leon Higdon

"The only qualification for admission to the pages of the Review will be—in the view of the Editors—either distinction of individuality or force of conviction . . . the criterion of inclusion being the clarity of action, the force or the illuminative value of the views expressed" [1]—so wrote Ford Madox Ford in a circular advertising the founding of the *English Review* in 1908, a review which in its first eighteen months would present to its readers two books by H. G. Wells, one by Joseph Conrad, four Thomas Hardy poems, four Henry James stories, as well as poems, stories, and essays by such individuals as John Galsworthy, D. H. Lawrence, Ezra Pound, William Butler Yeats, George Moore, Norman Dougals, E. M. Forster, Rupert Brooke, and even William Howard Taft—"an extraordinary achievement at any time". [2] Undoubtedly, the most significant novel the review

*Reprinted from *Review of English Studies,* n.s., 39, no. 154 (1988): 1–14. The research for this essay was made possible by a Travel to Collections Grant from the National Endowment for the Humanities.

published in its early years was Conrad's *Under Western Eyes,* serialized in eleven installments between December 1910 and October 1911.[3]

During the last twenty-five years, understanding of the relationship between the *English Review* serialization of this novel and the Methuen first edition has become confused because of a number of erroneous assumptions and some misinformation concerning Conrad's habits of composition and revision during this key transitional period of his career. Because these errors have perpetuated themselves in the scholarship and criticism, Conrad's style of revision and his several interventions in the text have been obscured. Both major biographers, Frederick R. Karl and Zdzislaw Najder, for example, have maintained that the first edition is "about 30,000 words fewer than the serial text,"[4] thus implying that major revisions, involving much cutting, occurred at some point between serialization and the publication of the book on 5 October 1911. Conrad himself also indirectly contributed to the misunderstandings, because critics have assumed that he accomplished what he intended when he wrote to J. B. Pinker: "I shall send you on Monday the text as published in the *ER,* torn out of the numbers and arranged for the printers. I wish Methuens to set up from *that.* There would be then no author's alterations—only corrections of misprints."[5] This letter has led critics to assume direct lineage between the two texts with revised pages of the one being used as setting copy for the other. One is encouraged to assume the truth of this because the closest students of the text, Roderick Davis and Emily Dalgarno, have stated that the differences between the two states are "very minor," "lightly scattered," and show signs of being only "slightly revised throughout."[6] Finally, all scholars have directly or indirectly subscribed to the "revision myth" which has Conrad completing the manuscript on 22 January 1910, suffering what we would today call an atypical depression for several months, and then revising the novel in April and May 1910. After all, we have Jessie Conrad's letter to David Meldrum, 6 February 1910, in which she unequivocally stated: "The novel is finished but the penalaty [*sic*] has to be paid. Months of nervous strain have ended in a complete nervous breakdown. . . . There is the M.S. complete but uncorrected and his fierce refusal to let even I touch it. It lays on a table at the foot of his bed and he lives mixed up in the scenes and holds converse with the characters."[7]

However attractive to and widespread in Conrad criticism these three assumptions may be, they must be discarded, because they simply do not agree with the evidence. First, and quite ironically, the serial and the book consist of exactly the same number of words, though not always the same words—113, 158 tokens—because while Conrad's revisions deleted 384 words from the text, they also added 384 words.[8] The serial and the book do differ a number of times: there are 394 verbal variants or substantives and some 1,253 punctuation and spelling or accidental variants between the two texts, but there was simply no extensive cutting done between the two texts. Indeed, Conrad told John Galsworthy late in 1911 that the book should have been and, if he had not been ill, would have been much longer than the serial: "You know, [he wrote to his friend] there are almost 30,000 words more [in the manuscript] than the printed text. Revising while ill in bed, I am afraid I have struck out whole pages recklessly. . . . There are passages which should have remained. I wasn't in a fit state to judge them. Well, it's done now, and let the critics make what they can of it."[9]

Second, something disturbing to Conrad occurred during Methuen's setting of the text. Conrad wrote to Warrington Dawson, almost six weeks after publication: "I am now having a row with Methuen about certain matters connected with the publication of that miserable novel of mine. I have been so outspoken with that beastly firm."[10] As early as 13 September, Conrad had mentioned the "Methuen muddle" to Pinker.[11] Among other things, Methuen had not liked the novel's title, feeling that it suggested "a book of descriptive impressions,"[12] but Conrad was more troubled by something in the proofs. He wrote to Pinker:

> It's true that in the first moment of irritation at such an instance of carelessness I told them that I would not return the proofs in hand til I had a complete set in my possession;

> but the very next day (at their request) I returned the first batch and the day after the whole lot right up to the page where the omission occurred. . . . As far as you are concerned I must say that all through you have done everything possible to spare me all the extra trouble in revising both text and proof.[13]

Obviously somehow the smooth progression from serial to marked pages to book had gone awry. Because the two texts differ so extensively in matters of spelling, hyphenation, and punctuation, one must at least entertain the possibility that the texts are not lineal in descent but rather radiate from a common source styled two different ways. Finally, as will be seen later, when Conrad completed the novel on 22 January 1910, he had already extensively revised the first two parts and had initially revised Parts Three and Four. The revisions which occurred during the spring of 1910 were a third round of revision to be followed by yet two more layers of revision, one of them possibly not by Conrad.

It has been necessary to clear the ground, so to speak, in order that the evidence gleaned through collation of the serial against the first edition, study of unpublished letters, and discovery of the marked typescript,[14] which disappeared following the 1928 Edward Garnett sale, can reveal precisely how Conrad approached his text between January 1910 and September 1911 and can demonstrate precisely why Conrad told Garnett "I had to work like a coal miner in his pit quarrying all my English sentences out of a black night."[15]

Statistics lay bare much of the story the variants have to tell, because they show that over half the substantive differences appear in Part Four of the novel (the parts are approximately equal in length[16]); moreover, tracing variants simultaneously forward through the printed texts and backward through the prepublication states shows two clear layers of revision, one completed before serialization and publication of the first edition, two stages of revision which differ quantitatively and qualitatively.

Obviously, at this stage in the evolution of his text, Conrad

Table 11.1: Distribution and Types of Verbal Variants

Part	Revision	Addition	Deletion	Total
1	40	5	8	53 (13.45%)
2	45	10	12	67 (17.01%)
3	44	11	9	64 (16.24%)
4	114	56	40	210 (53.30%)
Total	243 (61.68%)	82 (20.81%)	69 (17.51%)	394

was no "slash-and-burn" reviser as he was in the manuscript and early typescript stages. Instead, the raw figures shown in Tables 11.1 and 11.2 give us an image of a writer whose favored mode of revision was rewriting or reshaping an existing phrase, clause, or sentence, sometimes by adding or deleting a word or phrase. The figures also show that he considered Part Four far less polished than the rest of the novel. This is to be expected because he had revised Parts One and Two off and on since their initial composition between December 1907 and September 1908, whereas Part Four had been written between November 1909 and January 1910.[17]

The statistics do not reveal, however, the differences in the quality of the revisions. The 145 verbal variants unique to the *English Review* text, setting it apart from both typescript and first edition, are noticeably cautious in nature and, for the most part, involve rectifying grammatical niceties, correcting minor details, excising certain words or phrases such as "protest" and "that last," and replacing words with almost exact synonyms. Rarely do the variants have any particular significance. These revisions might possibly have been made by Robert Garnett rather than Conrad who "had agreed to read over and correct the clean final copy."[18]

In Parts One, Two, and Three, for instance, the only revisions which have more than a passing interest are those of "consciously" (S329.3) to "conscientiously" (1E62.2), a probable missetting; "invisible" (S689.18) to "invincible" (1E142.25); the deletion of the narrator's dismissing Razumov's suicidal

Table 11.2: Distribution of Variant Agreement

Part	TS/ER agree*	ER unique
1	32 (12.85%)	21 (14.48%)
2	57 (22.89%)	10 (6.90%)
3	57 (22.89%)	7 (4.83%)
4	103 (41.37%)	107 (73.79%)
Total	249 (63.20%)	145 (36.80%)

*TS = typescript; ER = *English Review.*

tendency—"Though he leaned dangerously far over the parapet, he had not the aspect of a man unduly fascinated by the suggestion of running water" (S100.20–2/1E194.33)—at the end of Part Two; and the phrase "lips moved" (S292.36) which became the Latinate "lips vaticinated" (1E220.11) in a restoration of an earlier manuscript reading. The others involve verb tense changes, the sharpening of idiomatic phrasing, selection of a more exact pronoun reference, the move from "further" to "farther," and several corrections of Sophia "Semenovna" to Sophia "Antonovna" to avoid the all too present allusion to Dostoevsky's *Crime and Punishment* in which Sophia Semenovna is a central character.[19] These are precisely the types of minute changes and corrections the friend of an author would feel comfortable making in a text, or the type of changes which might be made by a tired, troubled author embroiled in a 113,000-word novel he had intended to be only a 6,000 to 8,000 word short story.

The revisions made after Conrad received the *English Review* copy and was preparing the text for book publication are bolder, involving changes of details and recasting of significant phrases. A number of these changes remain indifferent in their effect, but phrases in Part One such as "many years" (S130.44), "gouty subject" (S136.22), "to mutter shyly" (S138.40), "whistling to" (S148.31), "strange scene" (S149.12), "on signing" (S159.41), and "brutally" (S335.39) became "a long time" (1E2.12), "gouty invalid" (1E10.2), "to murmer shyly" (1E13.19), "chirruping to" (1E27.14), "weird scene" (1E28.8), "on crossing" (1E43.13), and "roughly" (1E71.28). Usually, Conrad has selected the more precise, the more specific, word. "Chirrup," for example, describes more exactly the type of sounds a driver makes to his horses, and "crossing" would have been more immediately visualized by Conrad's largely Christian audience than "signing." Then, too, "murmur" accords better with "shyly" than does "mutter" with its hint of petulance. It is obvious that replacing "said in a gloomy murmur" (S144.27) with "said gloomily" (1E21.24) and "he said to himself" (S154.34) with "he reflected" (1E36.1) condense and tighten phrasing.

This pattern holds throughout Parts Two and Three as well, except that in Part Two, the "parapet" sentence was deleted, indicating that many, perhaps all, of the early changes originated with the author. (The "parapet" sentence may be of considerable importance. It first appears as a holograph addition to the typescript, and it is just possible that Conrad added it to the *English Review* while reading proofs against the typescript.) Conrad further decided to change Razumov's suit from "dark grey" (S74.20) to "dark brown" (1E157.28), to revise "protested" (S690.32, 691.5, 694.16, 695.26) to "explained" (1E144.18), "declared" (1E145.2), "assure" (1E149.26), and "said" (1E151.32).[20] Elsewhere, he deleted "their expression was that of quiet conviction" (S690.44–691.1/1E144.32) from a description of Natalia's eyes and "the only bit of colour she had" (S86.38–9/1E175.24) from a description of Madame de S——'s lips and finally to reverse "Succeed" (S698.13) to "Failed to" (1E155.16). In Part Three, Conrad decided Madame de S——'s voice was not "harsh" (S286.17, 287.13, 287.20–1, 288.44) but rather was "grating" (1E211.1) and "rasping" (1E212.9, 212.18, 214.27), and such a loosely structured, vaguely uncertain sentence as "There was something mysteriously positive in their assertion which startled" (S451.35–6) could be tightened to "The mysterious positiveness of this assertion startled" (1E245.16). " 'Don't rail,' she checked him sharply" (S650.12) became Sophia's more commanding " 'Leave off railing,' she checked him explosively" (1E275.26), though an attempted revision was derailed by incorrect verb form: "motionless with the papers crushed in his hand" (S659.2–3) became—and for some inexplicable reason remained so until 1920—"motionless, the papers holding in his hand" (1E288.1–2).

In addition, there were two major deletions from Part Three. Since the early revisions in the manuscript, Conrad had pared down the more obvious parallels between the narrator and Razumov and suppressed comments relating to Razumov's journal. As a result, Conrad cut the narrator's meditation on journals, perhaps in a move to make his narrator more limited, less perceptive, more self-deluded about his true attraction to Razumov's story:

> At any rate, the sincerity of their self-revealing intention cannot be [questioned]. Out of these pages, summarising months here, detailing days there with an almost incredible precision, out of the record of contradictory, incoherent thoughts emerges struggling for existence both against truth and falsehood a personality rising to a symbolic significance by the revealing nature of its individual fate. (S286.33–9/1E211.18)

And at the very end of Part Three, he struck out a metaphor which would have been more appropriate to Marlow in his expansive moments; indeed, it is but one of a number of echoes from *Lord Jim*: "It is well known that the way of salvation is hard, darkened by the shades of error and made lonely to an independent traveller. Even they who travel in guided troops and caravans are but spared the terrors of isolation" (S659.20-4/ 1E288.23).[21]

Part Four, though, confronts the textual critic with very different problems, simply because of the greater number of variants. Conrad was preparing copy for two texts almost concurrently, reading proofs for the *English Review* approximately four to six weeks before the monthly issues appeared and then marking pages torn from these issues to be used as setting copy for Methuen (also for Harper's in the United States). In May 1911, Conrad wrote to Pinker: "The proofs for the July *ER* are now hanging over my head. I wish I could reach the half of the book without interruption of mood—but that's impossible. I shall send you the dup^te sheets without delay for Harpers,"[22] and in a letter of 17 June 1911, he told Pinker he had corrected proofs for the June installment sometime in May.[23] At the very end of June, he wrote to Pinker: "I send you 7000w. of Chance, and enclose the text of the ER from which Messrs Methuen may begin to set text up, continuing from the June N^o. and so on from the end."[24] From these comments, the revisions in Parts Three and, especially, Four as well as Methuen's initial typesetting may be rather precisely dated. Since Conrad received proofs some weeks before serial publication, he had proofed the first half of the novel by March 1911.[25] Parts Three and Four would have been marked between April and late August 1911, while he was busy with the composition of *Chance,* and all revisions for the last half of the first edition would probably have been made between June and August 1911.

The revisions made for the *English Review* cluster in Razumov's two confession scenes, and Conrad effected several major adjustments in the relationship between Natalia[26] and Razumov at this stage. He made two significant additions to the text. The first picks up the "haunting" motif from Part One and from Conrad's original outline of the novel and allows Razumov to realize that his love for Natalia cannot be fully voiced until he has come to terms with his betrayal of her brother: "It was she who had been haunting him now. He had suffered that persecution ever since she had suddenly appeared before him in the garden of the Villa Borel with an extended hand and the name of her brother on her lips" (S453.4/1E337.52–338.1). The second and longer edition involves the narrator's analysis of the origins of their love. Tinged faintly with irony and masking his own disappointment, the narrator's thoughts run thus:

> It was manifest that they must have been thinking of each other for a long time before they met. She had the letter from that beloved brother kindling her imagination by the severe praise attached to that one name; and for him to see that exceptional girl was enough. The only cause for surprise was his gloomy aloofness before her

> clearly expressed welcome. But he was young, and however austere and devoted to his revolutionary ideals, he was not blind. (S455.39/1E342.23–32)

This passage is no simple addition but instead is a complex reworking of a passage in the typescript cancelled before the *English Review* was set.[27] This further suggests that Conrad proofed copy against his reworked typescript. In any case, the passage considerably sharpens the reader's perception of the characters' relationship and makes the narrator even more akin to the hesitant J. Alfred Prufrock.

Much tinkering was done in the scene to sharpen detail. The presence of Victor Haldin becomes "like the revenge of the unknown" (S451.40/1E335.28–9); Razumov now tells Natalia "'I always *did*'" (S453.1/1E337.28), speaking "as if in despair" and thus intensifying the extent to which he has understood but refused to recognize this awareness of the consequences of his act from the first. Natalia now responds "with earnest serenity" (1E341.12) rather than "with grave ardour" (S455.5), thus maintaining her regal, cool distance with no touch of attending passion. Again and again, Conrad heightens the sense that Razumov is discovering while in the act of confessing, and he added a touch of masochism with a simile which describes this act being "as though he were turning the knife in the wound and watching the effect" (S457.41/1E346.13–15). Conrad also heightened the estranged distance between the two, making Natalia less aware of implications. He had several times called her "visionary," but to one of these he added "under the spell of her own dread of lonely days, in their overshadowed world of angry strife, she was unable to see the truth struggling on his lips" (S459.34/1E349.20–3). And he could not resist underlining the melodramatic symbolism of having Razumov send his journal to Natalia "wrapped up in [her] veil" (S472.22/1E371.15) which Razumov had earlier taken.

Many of the revisions obviously seemed necessary to Conrad at the time but appear indifferent to the reader now. It seems to make no difference whether Mrs. Haldin's face is described as "white" (S451.20) or "bloodless" (1E335.1), whether Razumov entertained an "infamous purpose" (S463.7) or an "infamous intention" (1E355.20), whether he "fainted" (1E366.6–7) or "lost consciousness" (S469.20–1) after being struck by the tram, or whether Sophia "handed" (1E374.24) or "returned" (S474.20–1) the journal to the narrator after having read its pages "greedily" (1E374.23) or "avidly" (S474.20). Conrad's usual desire for tight, active phrasing was momentarily lost several times, as when "the breathlessness of his utterance contrasted" (S453.45) was revised to "There was a breathlessness in his utterance which contrasted" (1E339.16), and most readers will regret that Nikita's sinister and totally characteristic "He! He! He!" (S470.3) giggle becomes the more open and expansive "Ha! Ha! Ha!" (1E367.8).

The revisions made before the *English Review* publication are of a kind with the earlier typescript revisions: considerable tightening of phrasing, rather indifferent substitutions in a number of instances, some further corrections of phrasing and idiom, and a large handful of fairly significant changes, though Conrad is as likely to strike a telling adjective as he is to add one in this stage. He decided to cut "cutting its unpaved roadway through a dark wilderness of waste ground" (S317.20–1/1E328.30) from the description of a Geneva street and "black smudgy" (S317.31/1E329.8) from the description of a cheap newspaper, but, on the other hand, the thunder clouds of the last scene acquired an "awful blackness" (S318.27/1E330.16), and Natalia's "grace" (S456.65) became "seductive" (1E343.12). His extreme concern for *le mot juste* may be glimpsed when he revised "subtle official" (S94.40) to "faithful official" (1E301.15) to remove any hint of sly duplicity from one's understanding of Mikulin, changed "gentle" (S313.10) to "rich" (1E323.2) in describing Natalia's voice, shifted "defined" (S318.26) to "outlined" (1E330.14) when describing a person faintly seen in near darkness, emended "steady stare" (S318.28–9) to "weary stare" (1E330.17–18), more in keeping with the overall tone of the novel, and revised "horrible expressionless" (S460.7) to "appalling expressionless" (1E350.13) to intensify the shock of awareness rather than the ugliness of it. Equally revealing are several cuts, including "Planned as an attempt to seize power, it was to break out at a great review" (S315.6–8/1E325.24), thus detaching the action of the novel even further from its historical sources, and "the destructors should be anonymous" (S315.43/1E326.30), a virtual impossibility in this novel's world.

After all 394 of the variants have been scrutinized and thoughtfully considered, three conclusions can be reached concerning Conrad's habits during the revising and editing stages of composition. Conrad was a parsimonious writer who much preferred to adapt and readjust a sentence rather than to discard it, or to add more than a few words to it. Second, he effected no major structural rearrangements or character redefinitions in this stage but rather concentrated on sharpening existing phrases and clarifying, often highlighting, character relationships. Third, his hand was not always successful in improving his text but sometimes ensnared him in unidiomatic phrasing and flabby sentences—but rarely so—even at times in revealing reversals as when he revised "Pfui" (S475.44) to "Tfui!" (1E377.9), the opposite of "Tfui!" (S147.41) to "Pfui!" (1E26.11) early in Part One.

One central question, perhaps a most significant one, remains. Was Conrad's stated intention concerning the transmission of the text honored by Pinker and Methuen? Is the *English Review* text the direct progenitor of the Methuen? If it is, the Methuen typesetters exercised considerable freedom with the punctuation of the text, so much so, that it is obvious they imposed their own house styling. They may even have set from a duplicate typescript and have entered Conrad's revisions as the *English Review* pages reached the office. As mentioned earlier, the punctuation and spelling of the texts differ in 1,253 instances, an average of 3.32 times per page, and a glance at any Conrad manuscript, typescript, or marked proofs reveals that Conrad paid no consistent, systematic attention to either spelling or punctuation. At one point in handling *Chance*, Methuen wrote to Pinker: "Some of the chapters are punctuated with obvious care and with Conrad's characteristic precision, but the punctuation of other chapters is inconsistent with this."[28]

While the substantive variants show Conrad striving to pol-

Table 11.3: Distribution of Accidental Variants

Part	Number	Percentage	Average per page
1	294	23.46	3.03
2	253	20.19	2.61
3	320	25.45	3.40
4	386	30.81	4.34
Total	1,253		3.32

ish his sentences to a hard brilliancy through progressive stages of revision, the 1,253 accidentals tell a much different story whose underlying theme indicates that the punctuation and spelling of the *English Review* are the more Conradian. Although the book may be the text Conrad wished finally established, the book has moved far away from Conrad's usual practice in its accidentals, so much so that one must conclude exactly the opposite of Dalgarno, who wrote "nor can the text of the serial be considered authoritative, despite Conrad's statement, since diction was slightly revised throughout, several paragraphs combined or divided, and several minor passages added to the final installment before publication in book form."[29] That the new styling did not originate with Conrad can be demonstrated in several ways. If it did, one would expect to find a correspondence between the numbers of accidentals and the pattern clearly revealed by the substantives, with Part Four showing a greater number of variants. This, however, is not the case; rather, one sees a fairly steady ratio amongst the four sections of the novel. Because the accidentals, unlike the substantives, are evenly distributed, with no imbalance in the figures, the accidentals are far more likely to have originated with a hand other than Conrad's. It is most unlikely that Conrad would be using one system of punctuation early in 1910 and a very different one later in the same year. Moreover, if one turns to the typescript, one discovers a high degree of correspondence between the punctuation of the typescript and the serial, so high as to make it evident that the printers carefully followed their copy in the case of the magazine.

Table 11.4: Typescript and *English Review* Agreement

Part	Variants	TS/ER agree	Percentage
1	294	224	76.19
2	253	169	66.80
3	320	228	71.25
4	301*	152	50.50

*There is no typescript for pp. 366–77 of the text; therefore, the figures for Part Four are less than those in Table 11.3.

The close ties between the typescript and the *English Review* are evident in both small and large details. For example, the *English Review* and the typescript consistently use "western" where the Methuen edition uses "Western"; similarly "Mother," "newcomer," *"der Herr,"* and, in the later parts, "Petersburg" become "mother," "new-comer," "Der Herr," and "St. Petersburg" in the Methuen.[30] Methuen consistently expands the abbreviation "Mme." to "Madame." Both "silver medal" and "Silver Medal" appear in the serial; the Methuen reverses the typescript in both instances, capitalizing the typescript's lowercase "silver medal" and vice versa.

Larger patterns quickly emerge, making the book a far more heavily and rhetorically punctuated text than any previous form of the novel. The *English Review* and the typescript use *-ise* spellings (53 times) where the Methuen uses *-ize* spellings; where the serial uses a colon to introduce direct address set apart as a separate paragraph (135 times), Methuen uses a dash. Many, many more commas appear in the Methuen than in the *English Review* (444 more), and a number of times exclamation marks (8 times), periods (21 times), and commas (14 times) are changed to question marks.[31] There can be little doubt that someone—either Robert Garnett (unlikely) or someone at Methuen (more likely)—restyled the novel. Conrad himself was aware of some difficulties posed by his text, but he exaggerated when he told Galsworthy, "there was a good many phrases without grammar and even without sense."[32] Whatever the source, a uniform and consistent system of spelling, capitalization, and punctuation was imposed on Conrad's text, a system which would be preserved in the later English and American editions even though it bore no relationship to Conrad's lighter, looser, and generally satisfactory system. Methuen's action was comparable to the heavy varnishing galleries and museums often used on paintings.

The *English Review* text of *Under Western Eyes* gives us a unique opportunity to look at Conrad's habits of revision during a most troubling period of his career as he sought "the right word and the right accent" with which he "could move the world."[33] It also enables us to see how closely the stages of authorial composition, revision, and editing coexisted at this time and just how contaminated a text from this period tended to become once it reached any form of print. Because the years 1910 and 1911 are so crucial to Conrad's life and art, the more we know in detail about his working habits during this period, the more informed—and hence sounder—will be the conclusions we reach concerning both his life and his art and the need for him to write to a friend, saying, "I feel like a man returned from hell and look upon the very world of the living with dread."[34]

NOTES

1. Quoted in Arthur Mizener, *The Saddest Story: A Biography of Ford Madox Ford* (New York: World, 1971), p. 166.

2. Ibid., p. 170.

3. The text, hereafter abbreviated S (for serial), appeared as follows: Vol. 7 (1910), 130–65 (Dec.), 321–44 (Jan.), 507–29 (Feb.), 671–99 (Mar.); Vol. 8 (1911), 74–100 (Apr.), 275–303 (May), 444–63 (June), 640–59 (July); Vol. 9 (1911), 86–102 (Aug.), 305–19 (Sept.), and 449–76 (Oct.). The final installment is printed in eight-point type, whereas the first ten use ten-point type. The novel was published on 5 October 1911 by Methuen (London), hereafter abbreviated 1E (first English).

4. Frederick R. Karl, *Joseph Conrad: The Three Lives* (New York: Farrar, Straus & Giroux, 1979), p. 703; Zdzislaw Najder, *Joseph Conrad: A Chronicle* (New Brunswick, N. J.: Rutgers University Press, 1983), p. 574, n. 86. This assumption stems from a misunderstanding of Conrad's 15 October 1911 letter to John Galsworthy; see n. 9 below.

5. Quoted in Roderick Davis, "*Under Western Eyes:* 'the most deeply meditated novel,'" *Conradiana* 9 (1977): 73.

6. Ibid., p. 73, and Emily K. Izsak [Dalgarno], "*Under Western Eyes* and the Problems of Serial Publication," *RES*, n.s., 23 (1972): 436.

7. William Blackburn, ed., *Joseph Conrad: Letters to William Blackwood and Davis S. Meldrum* (Durham, N. C.: Duke University Press, 1958), p. 192.

8. The number is taken from David Leon Higdon and Todd K. Bender, *A Concordance to Conrad's Under Western Eyes* (New York: Garland, 1983), p. viii.

9. G. Jean-Aubry, *Joseph Conrad: Life and Letters* (Garden City, N. Y.: Doubleday, 1927), 2:136. Conrad also comments, "The other day I looked at the Ms.—1357 pp. averaging about 120 words per page." Conrad's figures are optimistically generous as this would have given him a 162,840-word text, a length never realized by the novel. The major cancellations in the manuscript (pp. 449–82, 506–40, 579–619) total only approximately 9,020 words. For these canceled passages, see my "Conrad's the Unkindest Cut: The Deleted Scenes of *Under Western Eyes*," *Conradiana* 19 (1987): 167–87.

10. Dale B. J. Randall, *Joseph Conrad and Warrington Dawson: The Record of a Friendship* (Durham, N. C.: Duke University Press, 1968), p. 144.

11. Conrad to Pinker, 13 September 1911. This and subsequent unpublished letters to Pinker, as well as those between Pinker and Methuen, are quoted with permission of the Joseph Conrad Estate and the Henry W. and Albert A. Berg collection, The New York Public Library, Astor, Lenox, and Tilden Foundation.

12. Methuen to Pinker, 11 July 1911. On 17 July, Methuen wrote to Pinker about omitting *Under* "so that the title now reads 'Western Eyes.'" Conrad, of course, did not agree, and in July informed Pinker, "Methuen might have spoken about the title ten months ago. They knew the book then. Now I have established the text in the *ER*. And the text includes the title which must stand." He did give permission for Methuen "to put *A Novel* in sub-title . . . with my blessing."

13. Conrad to Pinker, 13 September 1911.

14. See my forthcoming study, "The Typescript of Conrad's *Under Western Eyes*."

15. Conrad to Garnett, 28 August 1908, in *Letters from Joseph Conrad 1895–1924*, ed. Edward Garnett (Indianapolis: Bobbs-Merrill, 1928), p. 214.

16. The parts are respectively 97, 97, 94, and 89 pages in length.

17. See n. 14 above.

18. Najder, p. 683.

19. The presence of Semenovna in the manuscript has previously been noted by Dalgarno, p. 438; see also Eloise Knapp Hay, *The Political Novels of Joseph Conrad* (Chicago: University of Chicago Press, 1963), pp. 301–6.

20. "Protest" in its various forms remains in twenty-five instances in the novel; see Higdon and Bender, p. 203. For a similar example involving Conrad's awareness of his overuse of "sudden," see David Leon Higden, Floyd Eugene Eddleman, and Robert W. Hobson, "The First Editions of Joseph Conrad's *Almayer's Folly*," *Proof 4* (1975): 97–8.

21. See Conrad, *Lord Jim*, ed. Thomas Moser (New York: Norton, 1968), p. 131. For an even more striking example, consider "He was as lonely in the world

as a man swimming in the deep sea" (1E8.30–2) and its relationship to the "destructive element" passage in *Lord Jim,* p. 130.

22. Conrad to Pinker, [?] May 1911.

23. Conrad to Pinker, 27 June 1911.

24. Conrad to Pinker, Thursday, [?] June 1911.

25. Part One and the first section of Part Two appeared in the December 1910–February 1911 issues, with the remainder of Part Two appearing in the March and April 1911 issues. Part Three ran in the May, June, and July issues, with Part Four being published in the August, September, and October issues.

26. There is some confusion in the criticism as to whether Miss Haldin is Natalia or Nathalie. She is called Natalia (50 times), Nathalie (14 times), and Natalka (3 times) in the novel and the shift from Nathalie to Natalia probably represents both a change of mind on Conrad's part and a failure to resolve the inconsistency. *Natalka* is a diminutive form used only by her mother: *Nathalie* appears only in Parts Two and Three, being used by the narrator 13 times and Tekla once. *Natalia* is used throughout Parts Two and Three by Peter Ivanovitch (9 times) and in Part Four by Laspara (2 times), Razumov (13 times), and the narrator (26 times). If the narrator did not use two forms, the use of the various names would have some significance.

27. The typescript passage reads: "and it was impossible to imagine that the two women should have been kept out of the intercourse between such intimate political friends. And if he was at all attached to that friend, if he had any admiration for his character, it was enough to guide his thoughts to that friend's sister. She was no stranger to him when he saw her first: and to see that . . . " (TS S10–11), quoted with permission of the Joseph Conrad Estate and the Philadelphia Free Library.

28. Methuen to Pinker, 30 October 1912.

29. Dalgarno, pp. 436–37.

30. The examples cited are representative. I see no reason to list all instances of western/Western or newcomer/new-comer. Should one wish, they can be checked quickly through use of the concordance.

31. Other changes include adding commas (87 times), deleting hyphens (21 times), lengthening ellipsis marks (25 times), deleting abbreviations (45 times), capitalizing (25 times), lowering capitals (19 times), regularizing *anyone, everyone,* and *someone* (27 times), etc.

32. Quoted in Karl, p. 683.

33. Conrad, *The Mirror of the Sea and A Personal Record,* ed. Morton Dauwen Zabel (Garden City, N. Y.: Doubleday, 1960), p. 186.

34. Conrad to Henry Davray, 28 June 1910; quoted with permission of the Joseph Conrad Estate and the Humanities Research Center, University of Texas at Austin.

Conclusion

Betrachtungen eines Uneditorialischen; or Editorial Thoughts of an Uneditorial Man

John R. Reed

Joyce Carol Oates began her 1987 Hopwood Address at the University of Michigan by observing that whereas delivery is an obvious and verifiable event in literary as in biological creativity, gestation remains a secret and hidden program.[1] The secrecy of gestation is particularly bedeviling for editors who must deal with texts that are notoriously reserved about their antecedents. I admire and appreciate the work of editors who establish "definitive" texts and who chart the "biographies" of texts because my own scholarship requires such trustworthy documents upon which to make critical assessments. But I am also a sceptic because I am not convinced that the temporal linearity that most textual editors take for granted is a safe bedrock upon which to construct the temples of literary texts.

Here is my picture of the textual editor's dilemma. He or she has a major body of textual material to assemble in a rational way. Texts of various kinds are available, so an ordering principle is required and it is frequently a chronology. A poem, for example, was written, rewritten, printed, revised, and published. The sequence is clear. The obvious approach is to track the changes from version one, to version five, to version twelve of a text. Complicating such simple textual sequences are the nuisance accounts of witnesses to the text's evolution. Perhaps a friend heard the poem read in manuscript and his or her account does not coincide with any manuscript or printed version of the poem. Perhaps further the friend not only remembered and paraphrased the poem but actually transcribed a version of it that survives nowhere but in his or her private letters or memoirs.[2]

But this is a simple difficulty. At least the temporal placement of the friend's audience of the poem is possible and his or her rendering of the poem is testable against other temporally located texts. The real complication begins as we gradually depart from the world of texts. I won't mention here the problem that editors encounter when they realize that the author to whose work they are devoting such care burned pounds and pounds of manuscript evidence that *might* have clarified many a textual mystery. An editor could rightly view such an action as a species of authorial terrorism, a gesture designed to force the editor into accepting an "authorized" text.

Because they are documentable deletions from the history, or biography, of the text, these issues are rather minor compared with other, more secretive, details of literary gestation. What makes a sceptic like me uneasy are the atemporal possibilities of authorial secrecy. Let me begin gradually. Authors like Norman Mailer or Charles Reade have kept elaborate card files or notes for some of their novels. The materials that an artist accumulates for his or her work may be traceable insofar as we know roughly when they were gathered or how they were catalogued, but we can never be certain how they entered the author's creative track. A given character, incident, or idea appearing in the author's file may not appear in a finished novel, but that does not mean it did not at some time find its way into a projected, unrecorded, or unpreserved version of the story. Nor does it mean that some item in the notes did not trigger a now unrecognizable corollary in the finished story. One of the most intriguing traceable instances of this procedure is the record of musical sketches that eventually became Beethoven's Fifth Symphony.

Thomas Hardy's poetic career presents yet another dilemma. Hardy was writing poetry and making notes for poems from the 1860s on, though he published few and finished composition of only a handful, yet many years later he began to mine his notes, bringing out several volumes of poems that drew upon inspirations recent and remote. In this instance, it is possible to recover the stimuli for poems but impossible to know how the old Hardy reinterpreted the notes and drafts jotted down by the young Hardy. Still, this tracing of raw material, though it traverses time lines in a curious way, remains temporal in the usual linear sense. Other documents, such as letters or recorded conversations, can help to interpret Hardy's cast of mind when he made the notes and again when he utilized them for his poetry.

In her Hopwood lecture, Joyce Carol Oates noted how difficult it is to understand the energizing forces that prompt literary creation and instanced Yeats's account of being haunted by the line "a terrible beauty is born" after the Easter uprising in Dublin. We have no way of knowing how many possible contexts for this line were edited out before it achieved the status of the text he called "Easter, 1916."[3] Years ago in Storrs, Connecticut, I heard C. Day Lewis explain in an informal seminar that many of his poems came to him first devoid of text, simply as rhythms or metrical patterns charged with emotions. No editor in his or her right mind would seek to recover this pretextual information because without additional documentation commenting upon it, it offers no illumination. What kind of poem necessarily emerges from a trochaic hexameter line broken by a caesura?

Even when we have a text, it is not easy to comprehend its history, and yet editing is essentially a history of texts. Take the famous case of Tennyson's *Maud.* The poet had written in 1833–34 a lovely lyric poem that he called "Oh that 'twere possible," perhaps inspired by the loss of his friend Arthur Henry Hallam. Twenty years later, at the urging of a friend, Tennyson made this poem the germ of a much larger poem in a very different tone about a frenzied young man's love for a woman proscribed to him. Aubrey de Vere says that Tennyson set about making the poem intelligible by providing a preceding poem. "He wrote it; the second poem too required a predecessor; and thus the whole work was written backwards."[4] The history of this poem's creation is an abiding caution against too ready an assumption that literary artists have the same commitment to chronology that literary critics do. Moreover, Tennyson's revelation, when urged by Sir John Simeon to develop his lyric, that the poem "was really intended to belong to a dramatic poem which he had never been able to carry out," is another caveat.[5] An editor might assume that the dramatic poem Tennyson had in mind was substantially the same one that we now have in *Maud,* but there is no proof that this is the case. The concept of a dramatic setting may have been old, the story new—or some combination of these possibilities. Although editorial skills may trace the recorded stages of texts that survive and supplement their conclusions with anecdotal accounts, nothing certain can be known about the deletions and self-editings that do not survive. What a very different sort of poem *Maud* might seem if we did not know its secret history.

The situation is even more difficult when pre-texts are not transcribed until substantial portions of the composition in question are already completed. Anita Desai captures the poignancy of the unrecorded poem in her novel *In Custody* when the aged poet Nur entices the young scholar Deven with the promise of being permitted to transcribe the great man's unwritten poems. " 'I have many poems,' he muttered, with a certain slyness, 'many I could tell you—never written down, or written and lost. But I am too old to go hunting them down, too broken and crushed, you see, to find all that is there—somewhere here—' he slapped the side of his head, making it wag."[6] Wordsworth's brother explained that the poet "generally composed his verse out of doors."[7] Wordsworth himself indicated his distaste for partial composition in poetry. Working notes were all right for prose, he said, "but to write fragments of verse is an embarrassing practice. A similar course answers well in painting, under the name of studies; but in Poetry it is apt to betray a writer into awkwardness, and to turn him out of his course for the purpose of lugging on these ready-made pieces by the head and shoulders."[8] The modern editor lacks not only such heads and shoulders to seize upon but the rest of the torso as well if the whole process of composing, deleting, and rearranging goes on in the mind of the poet before a text is committed to paper. He is like the reader of Mary Shelley's *Frankenstein,* who is told about Frankenstein's gathering of limbs for his creature, but who has no clue to the method by which those parts were fused into a whole living being after all.

Tennyson's case resembles Wordsworth's. He too composed his poems in his head while he was out walking. As a young man he chanted them to the winds in a manner that made witnesses doubt his sanity.[9] John Pfordresher, the editor of *A Variorum Edition of "Idylls of the King"*, explains that "Tennyson was a poet who began to ply his pen only after a great deal of work was finished in his head." He would often brood on his poems for months. "Such a practice, of course, rules out false starts and half-formed conceptions appearing in manuscript. Since the work of shaping the outline of the whole was done within the mind, it is lost to posterity." To make things more difficult, "It seems evident from his notebook that he did not work through his poems from the first line to the last, creating them in sequence. Rather, he would work on whatever passage or scene seemed 'ready' for composition."[10] This mode of composing presents serious hazards for an editor. Suppose that the poet has composed a long section, let us say, of the *Idylls of the King,* but upon reflection, feels that parts of what he has fashioned are inappropriate and therefore does not transcribe them. Later, he returns to the notebook where he has written down his poem and decides that the excluded lines are appropriate after all and pens them in on a blank verso. An editor might feel reasonably safe in considering the added lines chronologically later and thus in the nature of afterthoughts. He or she cannot know, without external evidence, that these lines *precede* or are *coeval with* the text that was transcribed first. An editor has little choice but to assume that the history of transcription and the history of composition are basically the same. And yet, to so "historicize" the text is to invite misreadings simply through the channeling of the poet's genius into a temporal flow, with all its flotsam of causal implications.

Today we are moving into a world that will both simplify and complicate the editor's task. Computers are extremely handy for processing information and facilitating editorial operations, but they create a potential dilemma for future editors of texts now being generated. As writers become more accepting of word processors for their composing, the traces of their procedures will be increasingly detemporalized unless they make conscious efforts to maintain the history of their creative acts. An author may create a text on a computer, then delete and save a block in the same or in an altered form, or move any version of it to a new location in the text. No record of these actions would normally survive, and an editor would have no tools to recover the stages toward a final text. What I am suggesting here is that editors have to some degree always been faced with comparable problems. Committed to a "historical" approach to texts, they must often assume history where they have no evidence. This assumption may be unwarranted, but the evidence against the historical assumption is missing too because it never existed in recorded text but only in the minds of the authors themselves.

I cannot see that my comments will or should make any difference in the way editors operate. After all, they can work only with materials that have become decipherable texts. Where I might hope for some change is among the critics who employ editors' products. Editors know the dreadful pitfalls of their methods and generally remain humble before the impossible ideal of the Fully Authenticated Text. But critics are not so chastened by the effort of establishing texts and may be all too easily moved to a grand generalization or an interpretive gesture by what they perceive to be the confirmed protocol of a given text. If we recall that there is always an unrecorded pre-text for every text, and that creative effort in literature, unlike biological procreation, is not bound to a necessary temporal pattern, we may be more cautious in using a "definitive" version of a text as our own pretext for convenient critical assumptions.

NOTES

1. Joyce Carol Oates, "Beginnings," *Michigan Quarterly Review* 27 (Winter 1988): 2.

2. Something like this happened with Tennyson and his friends. Tennyson's Cambridge friend, J. M. Heath, kept a Commonplace Book in which he recorded many of Tennyson's poems. It remains a major resource for students of Tennyson's poetry.

3. Oates, p. 5.

4. Hallam Tennyson, *Alfred Lord Tennyson: A Memoir,* 2 vols. (New York: Macmillan, 1905), 1:379.

5. Hallam Tennyson, *Tennyson and His Friends* (London: Macmillan, 1911), p. 308.

6. Anita Desai, *In Custody* (Harmondsworth, England: Penguin, 1985), p. 88.

7. Ernest de Selincourt, ed., *The Letters of William and Dorothy Wordsworth: The Early Years, 1787–1805,* 2d ed., rev. by Chester L. Shaver (Oxford: Clarendon Press, 1967), p. 477.

8. Ernest de Selincourt, ed., *The Letters of William and Dorothy Wordsworth: The Middle Years, Part II 1812–1820,* 2d ed., rev. by Mary Moorman and Alan G. Hill (Oxford: Clarendon Press, 1970), pp. 178–79.

9. Hallam Tennyson, *Tennyson and His Friends,* p. 15.

10. John Pfordresher, *A Variorum Edition of Tennyson's "Idylls of the King"* (New York: Columbia University Press, 1973), pp. 13ff.

Index

Index

Index

A NOTE ABOUT THE EDITOR

Judith Kennedy received a Ph.D. in English Literature from New York University and currently teaches at Kutztown University. As an Associate Professor of English, she teaches graduate and undergraduate courses in Victorian literature, serves on the Honors Program Advisory Board, and has directed the Developmental Writing Program. She, her daughter, and Labrador retriever live in Allentown, where she writes articles on Tennyson, Hardy, Victorian culture, and the teaching of writing and literature.